surfers

surfers

A KIWI LIFESTYLE

Jo Caird and Paula George

Bateman

Text and Photography © Jo Caird and Paula George
Design and typography © David Bateman Ltd, 2015

Published in 2015 by David Bateman Ltd
30 Tarndale Grove, Albany, Auckland, New Zealand

www.batemanpublishing.co.nz

A catalogue record for this book is available from the
National Library of New Zealand.

ISBN 978-1-86953-922-1

Publisher: Bill Honeybone
Book design: Cheryl Smith, Macarn Design
All photographs (cover and internals) by authors except where indicated
Printed in China by Asia Pacific Offset Ltd

Contents

About this book

The desire to create this book was born from both Georgie (Paula George) and I falling in love with surfing. Relatively late starters, we discovered a world where people's lives literally revolved around the waves. Unlike most sports or hobbies, this one seems to encroach on every aspect of a surfer's lifestyle. The people we met were wonderfully diverse and we thought it would be a great idea to tell some of their stories.

Most of us know something about professional surfers through TV and social media, but less is known about the weekend warriors, the board shapers, the longboard collectors and those who just live for the next wave. What excites surfers? What motivates them to brave all kinds of weather in search of just one more wave? How has a passion for surfing affected the lives of the individuals in this book, and impacted on their families?

Surfers are indeed a diverse group, and the ocean levels the playing field. Out there, sitting on the water, it's hard to tell the company CEO from the tradesman, the mother, or even the toilet cleaner, and why would you want to? It's all about the surf.

It has apparently been scientifically proven that surfing makes you happier. Travelling around New Zealand and interviewing and photographing so many wonderful people for this book, we saw clearly how much joy each individual gets from simply being on top of a wave.

Technically, it has something to do with ionised water particles that surfers ingest or inhale as waves break, but it's also got plenty to do with the great memories created, the rich tapestry of people out there in the line-up or the car park, the feeling of accomplishing something new, or maybe even just the simple joy of riding a board along a surge of energy. Perhaps it's even the physical workout, merged with a meditation session, surrounded by nature. In any case, surfing seems to be able to make people feel 10 years younger with a single wave.

It is also true, however, that for every great ride there is a humbling tumble just around the corner. The learning curve is endless but with a reward so good that surfers always come back for more. It doesn't seem to matter how good the conditions are or how well you surf — just paddling out somehow makes the world seem a better place.

Kelly Slater has said, 'Surfing — it's like being in the Mafia. Once you're in, you're in. There is no getting out!' So often it's as simple as finding a clean green wave on a quiet beach somewhere. We are so fortunate that this is still a possibility in New Zealand, and both Georgie and I can't wait to share the love of surfing and being in the water with our children.

Jo

Andrew Earl-Peacock

An Enviable Quiver

Singer-songwriter and surfer Jamie McDell says, 'If I could be a guy, I would want to be Andrew Earl-Peacock. He's just such a cool dude.'

Andrew has long flowing hair, a body that has obviously spent hours surfing on the water, and a mellow attitude to match. Growing up, he spent every summer at Whangamata, in the water and on the beach. His introduction to surfing came from playing around on a boogie board, which he then learned to stand up on and ride. He bought his first real surfboard when he was 11. It's a 6 ft 8 in board with chillies painted around it, and he still has it. When he was a kid his favourite band was The Red Hot Chili Peppers so he feels a real attachment to the board and won't be parting with it.

He's also never far from his other pride and joy — his surfing van, a 2000 Toyota HiAce Super GL. The main reason he bought it was so he could take his longboards everywhere without having to strap them on the roof or cram them inside (meaning he couldn't take any

passengers). Plus it means he has comfortable accommodation while chasing surf around the country. Set up well enough to easily live in (which he did for seven weeks this year while doing late-season lifeguarding at Hot Water Beach), it has developed into his 'home away from home'. To date, the most boards he has carried in it is 13, and there was still heaps of room.

Just as well, as he has a massive collection from 5 ft 2 in boards up to 10 ft, all part of the communal family quiver. 'My older brother started scouting Trade Me and we began collecting them. We used to go and have family surfs with Dad, which was really awesome. Dad still gets out there occasionally, but usually it's just to keep me company.'

So much of Andrew's life is based around surfing. He makes his own clothes, as well as surfboard 'socks'. He works part-time at Pete Anderson's factory (see page 41), and loves being able to shape his own boards. 'It doesn't pay great and I'm never going to make a huge living out of shaping boards, but I get up every morning excited about the boards I'm going to repair and work on, so that's really cool.

'Surfing is just pure addiction. It's the last thing I think about when I go to bed at night and the first thing I think about when I wake up in the morning. I go out and surf and enjoy it, but as soon as I'm out of the water I'm thinking about the next one. It just ends up being such a big part of your life. I don't remember what it was to start with, but now I can't imagine my life without it.'

Ella Williams

World Junior Champion

As a four-year-old, Ella Williams rode her first wave. As an eight-year-old, she wrote on her bedroom wall that she wanted to be a world champion. As an 18-year-old, she was.

Ella's victory at the 2013 World Junior Surfing Championship in Brazil really was a remarkable, against-the-odds achievement. A last-minute call-up for the event, Ella had only a week to prepare and get herself to Brazil. Unlike all the other competitors who had a full entourage of coaches, managers and nutritionists, Ella had just her mum. Janine Williams is not your average mum, though. Along with her husband, Dean, she has been a massive supporter of Ella's surfing and loves riding the waves as much as her daughter.

It was because of her parents' love of surfing that Ella first stood up on a board aged four. Along with her brother, Braedon, Ella has been fortunate to have her whole family wanting to spend their spare time at the beach and riding waves.

Her dad, Dean, talks about tucking Ella into his wetsuit and heading out in Manu Bay. The Raglan of 20 years ago was very different from today, with no crowds and plenty of space for a young grom finding her way. Ella clearly remembers her bright-yellow togs, and jumping up on the front of her dad's Mini Mal while holding on to his hair.

In 2002, when Ella was seven years old, her parents bought the Whangamata Surf Shop, meaning Ella had the good fortune of growing up in one of New Zealand's iconic surfing towns. It is here that she perfected her craft and become one of New Zealand's most exciting young talents.

Ella entered her first surf competition at age six and clearly loves the competitive side of the sport. She is very clear about her goal to be the best female surfer in the world. She wants not only to win the Women's World Title, but to win it multiple times. It's a lofty ambition but given her love of the sport and her desire to push herself as far as she can, it appears to be an achievable one.

When thinking about her favourite place to surf, Ella straightaway mentions Whangamata. 'I've been to lots of great surf places around the world, but nothing beats home. We're lucky enough to have the Whangamata Bar pretty much on our back doorstep. It's a perfect left-hander; it's so much fun. When it's on, the wave is just world-class.'

But back to Brazil and the World Juniors.

'I was stoked to get into the quarters, and then to make it into the semi-finals was amazing! To make it into the final wasn't even in my wildest dreams, so when I got there I was just so happy. So proud of myself that I just thought I have nothing to lose and I should just be patient and wait for the waves to come. I had to wait a really long time, which was just so hard. It was all in the final eight minutes that I caught a couple of waves. It was crazy and I managed to get two good scores. I waited for confirmation that I had actually won before I let myself celebrate. It was the best day ever!'

Now Ella's spending time travelling around the world and trying to get enough points to qualify for the World Tour. She just needs a few good results and for things to go her way.

It's hard to mention Ella's name without people saying, 'Oh, the Junior World Champion. Isn't she amazing?'

And it's true. She is.

Image courtesy of Cory Scott.

Matt Scorringe

The Art of Surfing

For several years Matt Scorringe had been living the dream. Travelling the world on the World Pro Junior circuit, riding for Billabong as a free surfer being paid to travel the world with videographers and photographers, and then, finally, working with pro surfer Josh Kerr, travelling and filming him on the Pro circuit.

Life was amazing and always filled with adventure and possibilities, then, in January 2010, he was diagnosed with leukaemia. With his life turned upside down, Matt began chemotherapy the very same night he was diagnosed. Educating himself in nutrition and focusing on strengthening his immune system as much as he possibly could helped him feel as if he had some control over the situation, and that he was being proactive in his own treatment and recovery.

He credits his competitiveness in surfing and his love of being in the water with helping him face the challenge of cancer. He talks fondly of the doctors who allowed him to go for a surf at the halfway

mark of his treatment. 'They sort of want to build you up before they knock you down again.'

Hearing Matt talk about his first time back in the water makes you appreciate just how much surfing means to him. 'My first surf back was something I will never forget. Throughout my whole treatment the thought of being back in the water and back on my board was a massive drive to get through it all.'

The plan was to have his first surf on his 25th birthday, back in Whangamata with all his friends and family. But the day before his birthday, the Whanga Bar had these gorgeous little waves, only one guy was sitting out there, and Matt realised he just had to go out. So he did, and he had that special moment all to himself. The first wave ran off and he couldn't even keep up with it! He paddled out, with his partner, Casey, watching from the beach. She had been there every step of the way throughout his treatment so it just seemed right. He came back to the beach with an indescribable feeling of happiness, both from the feeling of surfing again, and also knowing he could still do it after everything he'd been through.

Competing since the age of 10, Matt's life had been driven by professional surfing. His main priorities had been keeping sponsors happy with imagery and surfing the right way to get good scores in competition. Surfing post-cancer was suddenly all about just the simple joy of surfing and being back in the water.

But Matt was determined to get back to the level he had been surfing at. A year after he was first diagnosed, he went to the Nationals. It was a personal challenge and, for the first time ever, he was just competing against himself.

Now a new father, Matt's priorities have changed again. He lives in Raglan, where he coaches surfing at the local Raglan Surfing Academy. This marries together perfectly with his own coaching development programme, 'The Art of Surfing'. Aimed at elite surfers and up-and-coming young surfers, his programme utilises a lot of film analysis, tactical advice and psychology. Matt travels all over the world — predominantly with groups of Russians who love spending time at Dubai wave pools, making the most of guaranteed waves in a controlled environment.

This past year, Matt was invited to be part of the New Zealand High Performance Sport coaching programme. 'Coaching Advance' is about educating the coaches across all sports. Sharing ideas and concepts with such a huge range of specialists in their sports has been invaluable. Now he can take it all back to his surf coaching. Upskilling himself and growing as a coach is all very much part of the immediate plan.

When asked what it is about surfing that draws him, Matt straightaway mentions the feeling of being barrelled. 'It's the most unbeatable feeling in the world being in a barrel, especially scary barrels — the adrenalin and the fear, followed by the reward. Nothing, absolutely nothing, beats it.'

Jay Jackman

Daily Practice for the Soul

Surfing is a funny thing, as Australian author Tim Winton writes in his novel *Breath*:

> *How strange it was to see men do something beautiful. Something pointless and elegant, though nobody saw or cared ... as if dancing on water was the best and bravest thing a man could do.*

These words have always struck a chord with board shaper Jay Jackman. He looks back to some of the old guys like Buttons Kaluhiokalani (the Hawaiian surf legend), saying, 'Those guys really could dance on water.' Sadhana, the name Jay puts on his surfboards, is Sanskrit for 'daily practice for the soul'.

He started shaping at around 12 years old when his dad said, 'If you want to ride them, you can fix them too.' So he fixed and shaped a few

boards before he started working at the board factories in Sydney off and on, while also working as a lifeguard for over 15 years.

Jay's parents both surfed, and his dad, Mick, taught Jay when he was five. His parents owned a surf shop in Newquay, England, during the halcyon days of the 1960s and '70s. Mick was an equally talented jazz pianist, as well as a composer and arranger, and, in his spare time, taught Jay how to make surfboards. He's stopped working now but music was his main job for 40 years. Jay considers him a complete genius. In the early 1980s, Mick wrote a song for one of New Zealand's foremost jazz vocalists, Malcolm McNeill (Ambrose McNeill's father — see page 139), which was recorded by Dame Kiri Te Kanawa's record label.

Mick also had a collection of old '60s and '70s surf magazines that Jay used to flick through as a kid, and he loved all those plane shapes and single fins even then. Big wave surfing was the thing, and big wave guns were the boards. Jay's making those now. They've become really popular again — almost mainstream. His love of the style has stood the test of time. Shaping goes around and keeps coming around. His uncle was a renowned big wave rider in the '60s; he was in that early crew that worked as stunt doubles for Hollywood actors in Waimea, Hawaii.

But Jay likes surfing the short, in-between retro boards, which the Japanese call transitional boards. 'They are a flat, fishy style — single-fin; they have a bit more of a soul feel to them. It feels as if you're on a snowboard, not just *bang, bang, bang*, all about the rip and turn.'

Having grown up in Narrabeen, he'd definitely done his time on the short performance board. One day, though, Jay and his wife got out a map and realised that neither of them had been to neighbouring New Zealand. They booked a 10-day holiday, and now it's home. 'We both love the mountains as well as the ocean so Christchurch is the perfect base. It has a good feel about it. There are some really good people here, plus the opportunity to snowboard and surf. Bonus.'

Sadhana Surfboards was started in 1997 as a reaction to the mass-market one-size-fits-all approach to surfing of the time. Drawing on the influence of the ocean, and using various shaping rooms and sheds around the world, the couple formed their label. While those backyard days are gone, it is the hand-made craft philosophy that still drives Sadhana to produce beautiful boards.

The company has grown to provide a comprehensive range of hand-shaped boards to suit all styles of surfing. A new board takes about six to eight weeks' turnaround. Sadhana Surfboards likes to get its boards out quickly. When setting up, Jay thought about how he wouldn't want to wait over three months for a new board. 'We have a great setup here now. All the people who work on the boards are local blokes, all surfers. It was hard through the quake period, as everything fell down and we didn't know what the future was going to be. The water was off limits for about nine months so we had to travel to surf. It seems like a long time ago now. Things are all good now, except the roads.'

Jay doesn't surf as much as he'd like to, but he doesn't need to get in the water twice a day every day. Well, not any more. He feels that having surfed for over 30 years, his time in the water has made him mellow. Christchurch is not blessed with consistent surf either so while accessibility is good, and it's uncrowded and friendly, the waves are not always there. So then he can work a day in the shaping bay. It's like a day at the beach — a noisy day, but at least he's making something. Jay needs that creative buzz.

'When I get out there now it's a wind-down; it grounds me. Sometimes I even just paddle out around the bays just for the quiet and for what you can see in the water. There are often little Hector's dolphins around. I guess I'm looking for more in my life than just the physical stuff.'

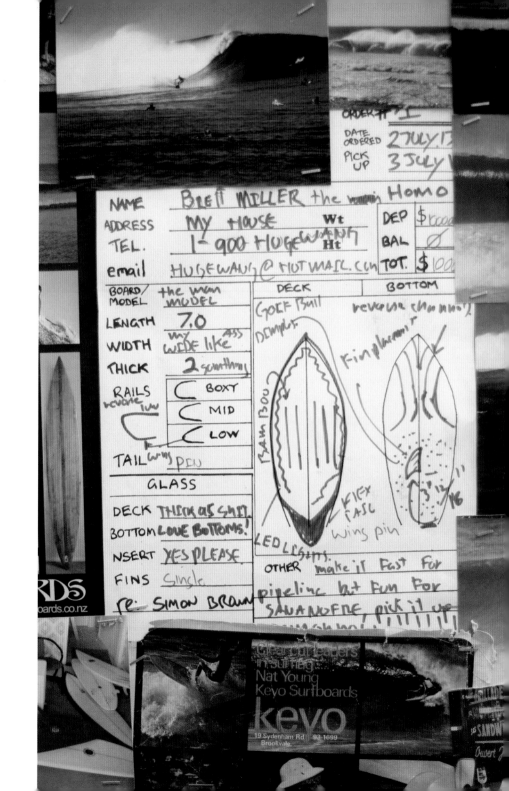

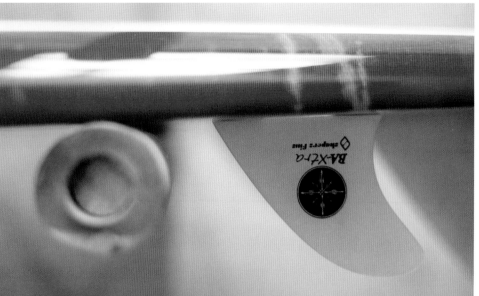

THE ONLY GOOD SUIT IS A WET SUIT

SHAPING CONSIDERATIONS

REMEMBER THAT WHEN YOU DO THE DECK, YOU WILL DESTROY THIS PAPER, SO TRY TO UNDERSTAND THE WHOLE THING NOW. FIRST THING IS **NOT** TO SKIN IT. IF I LEFT SOME LUMPS ON THE RAIL BANDS, TRIM THEM DOWN BEFORE **TEMPLATING**. BALLPOINT PENS SEEM TO WORK BEST. BECAUSE OF THE FOAM CORE THESE BLANKS OFFER LESS LATITUDE IN THE **LENGTH**. SO I DESIGN THE ROCKER TO BE ALL USED. DON'T CUT MORE THAN 1" OFF NOSE AND/OR TAIL. YOU CAN USUALLY **ADD** AN INCH OR 2 TO THE BLANK USING HARD WOOD **NOSE** & TAIL BLOCKS. **WIDTH** IS A SIMILAR STORY. THE MORE STRIPS YOU LEAVE ON THE RAILS (OF THE 4 ON EACH SIDE) THE MORE YOU CAN CROWN THE DECK AND ROLL THE RAILS. DON'T TAKE OFF MORE THAN 2 STRIPS (1½") EACH SIDE. **THICKNESS**: ONCE YOU'VE SETTLED ON A PLANSHAPE THAT'S COMPATIBLE TO THE BLANK, AND CUT IT OUT, TAKE A DEPTH GAUGE AND MAKE A WITNESS LINE (AGAIN BALLPOINT PEN) ON THE RAIL EDGE YOU JUST CUT OUT. ONE LINE SHOULD BE 20 mm (¾") DOWN FROM THE DECK SURFACE, TIP TO TAIL PORT & STARBORD. THE OTHER LINE IS 15 mm (5/8") UP FROM THE BOTTOM, ALSO ALL THE WAY AROUND THE BLANK. THESE TWO LINES SHOW YOU WHERE THE FOAM STARTS AS YOU ARE ADJUSTING ROCKER AND THICKNESS FOIL. **TOOLS**: THE HEAVIER THE PLANER THE BETTER, BOTH IN AMPS & WIDTH. I SWEAR BY MY ROCKWELL (14 YRS.) A REGULAR STANLEY-TYPE IRON CARPENTERS PLANE (IF YOU CAN WORK ONE) IS GREAT FOR KNOTS & RAILS & CONCAVES, BUT SO IS THE KIND THAT USE RAZOR BLADES. SANDING IS GREAT WITH #40 GARNET PAPER STUCK ON A 18" LONG BLOCK. I ALSO USE THIS SANDING BLOCK TO TOUCH UP ANGLES ON NOSE & TAIL BLOCKS. REMEMBER TO SAND EXACTLY **WITH THE GRAIN**. SMALL DEVIATIONS MAKE BIG SCRATCHES YOU DON'T SEE TILL **GLASSING**. BECAUSE OF DIFFERING WOOD POROSITIES, WE USUALLY PRIME THE BLANKS WITH POLYURETHANE VARNISH, AND DE-FUZZ THEM WITH #80-100. WE NEVER PUT MORE THAN SINGLE 4 OZ GLASS JOBS (MAYBE A DECK PATCH IF IT COMES OUT RIDICULOUSLY LIGHT). AND OURS TYPICALLY LAST 5 YEARS HERE IN TROPICAL-RESIN-EATING SUN & YEAR ROUND WARM WATER USAGE. WHICH IS A GOOD REASON NOT TO MAKE TOO TRENDY A BOARD. THAT GIMMICKY SHIT SHOWS UP YEARS LATER TO HAUNT YOU. STEP RIGHT UP AND WAIL US OUT A BEAUTY.

George Andus

Charlie Young

Living the Dream

With his long grey beard plaited into a pirate braid, it's hard to believe that this ageing surfer was once wearing a suit and tie and doing a desk job. Full of enthusiasm for anything to do with either surfing or Raglan, Charlie's story is one that gives hope to anyone who finds themselves stuck in the daily grind.

Charlie started off as a young punk growing up in Southern California, and he believes that discovering surfing at age 11 was a critical factor in his life. His teenage years were spent in the water and he qualified as a surf instructor before studying at San Diego State University, so chosen because it meant he could continue to surf. But reality hit home and he took the traditional route, ending up with a nine-to-five desk job.

Fast-forward to Charlie turning 40, and two airline tickets landing in his lap. He and his wife suddenly had the opportunity to travel as far as they wanted, so they literally decided to go as far as they could — to New Zealand. A friend had shown them a surf article about the

break known as 'Indicators' so they decided to start their trip in Raglan.

The plan was to travel the length of New Zealand, but, 35 days later, not only were they still in Raglan but they had purchased a house above Indicators. Charlie had quit his job of 20 years and, along with his wife, had put their restaurant back in San Diego on the market.

For Charlie it was a chance to flip the switch and start over again. They wanted to find a way to surf every day, to not have to work normal jobs, and to be able to live at Indicators 'because it's the coolest place in the world to live'. So they decided to start a surf school — the very first in New Zealand. In 1998, surf schools were working overseas but there was none in New Zealand, much less in Raglan.

Sixteen years later and all those ideas and enthusiasm have evolved into the Raglan Surf School and Karori Lodge, which provides accommodation for up to 75 people in the most picturesque of locations.

Still a mad keen surfer (until recently when he snapped his Achilles tendon), Charlie would usually surf every day. His bedroom overlooks the very break he read about in that magazine 20 years ago, and, as a goofy footer, it doesn't get much better than this left-hand, world-class point break. He has a real soft spot in his heart for the place, not just being able to surf such amazing waves but being out in the water with such high-calibre surfers. 'Watching them close up day in and day out — it's the ultimate.'

Surfing has kept Charlie moving in his life, giving him a pathway and opening doors. 'That serendipity that happens in your life when you follow your nose ...'

The couple did finally end up travelling around the South Island and discovered that the rest of the country is actually 'really cool!' But he reckons the connection with Raglan was immediate as they first drove over the hill into the seaside town. They book looked out and exclaimed 'Wow!'

Charlie is living his dream. 'We are the wealthiest people in the world because we are doing exactly what we want to be doing every single day.'

Daisy Day

A Daily Wave

Daisy started surfing comparatively late in life. Even though her family lived at the beach, her English parents wouldn't let her go down there.

When she was 16 years old, and unbeknownst to Mum, a friend took her on a motorbike down to the wild sands of Castlecliff, where they met a group of his mates who were surfing. Daisy thought, 'Oh my goodness, I am going to do this!' She had heard lots of songs about surfing while growing up so she already knew a bit about this soulful sport.

'In the water, on a surfboard, I still remember it. It was the end of summer and I had all the wrong gear on: shorts and a bikini top, and a T-shirt. It was absolutely brilliant.' That first ride was on a friend's board, but she recalls that her own first board was a 6-foot, single-fin Roger Titcombe board.

A new crew of girl surfers comes through every year so there is now more drive to compete and, of course, there's a lot more gear

available now — surf clothes and wetsuits made specifically for women. There are also boards that are a little bit wider and a little bit fatter, which suit women better because their paddling technique is different from that of the guys.

'Obviously, there is a place for competitiveness, but when girls free-surf they seem a lot more chilled out, not quite so flashy as the boys.' This statement may well get her in a bit of trouble with some of her male co-surfers but they would probably agree that adding just one woman to the line-up seems to bring a more chilled vibe to the session, making the boys far more talkative and just that little bit better behaved. Probably the most important thing is that Daisy feels girls have a bit more fun out there.

Daisy was in Hawaii last year and she thought she'd like to surf like the Hawaiians do. She loves the single-fin longboard because it's the traditional way of surfing. All the young girls there were surfing 9-foot and bigger boards. 'They are so stylistic, so beautiful.' She also liked the fact that there were a lot of older Hawaiian women out there — 'Wow, what grace!'

Formerly a senior photographer at the *Taranaki Daily News*, Daisy progressed through to middle management and, when the whole newspaper industry was starting to change, she decided it was a good time to move on and maybe take up surf coaching as she wanted to surf more anyway. Her husband, Arch (see page 131), was pleased for her except for those times when he'd come off his shift at the fire brigade and she'd tell him all about her fantastic session on 6-foot solid surf at Waiwhakaiho, and go into great detail about how brilliant it was.

Daisy loves coaching and watching her students getting buzzed out. Her coaching journey started when she saw girls being dragged out by their boyfriends into big waves. If she saw a girl floundering in the water, she would check she was okay and help out, and it started from there. The fact that the majority of Daisy's business comes through word of mouth is testament to how good she is as a coach.

She meets lots of people, of all ages. In the past five years she has even coached women over 60 — usually overseas visitors who just want to have a

go. She also had a regular customer who was over 70 — a pretty fit guy. She says surfing is actually easy on the body, and you should ride whichever board suits your age and ability.

Daisy has also always wanted to publish a book, and she had in mind to do one based on her news photography. She had also photographed a lot of surfing, and when others commented that she was a bit of a historian of the surfing community of Taranaki and she should publish her work, it dawned on her that she had, in fact, documented the 'Naki surf culture from the 1970s onwards. It was a book waiting to be published. So she dug out all her photographs and whittled them down to a 150-page book: *Daisy Day: 30 Years of Surf Photography*. It ends with a stunning series of portraits of surfing families. It's something she obviously wants to develop further and we may yet see a future project around surfers and their siblings.

Waiwhakaiho is Daisy's favourite place to surf. 'It's got long, long lefts, which I like, but it's also got beautiful right-handers. It's best in a big swell.' Daisy recalls her first time out there when there was a mountain of white

water, but she was determined to give it a go. It took her 35 to 40 minutes to get out. 'I saw the other guys, their heads anyway, and huge sets come marching through. It was maybe fifteen years ago and I'll always remember it. I was clawing and trying to get over the sets. I finally got a wave and it took me so far down that the paddle back would have been another forty minutes. I took the thirty-minute walk back instead.' So was it worth all that effort? 'Definitely! It was such a big swell that day, and later I talked to a couple of guys who were out there who said they'd been pretty jittery about the size of the waves.

'I just love the sea, the feel of it, the way the currents move, the smell of it ... it's always challenging because it's always different. When you're out surfing in Taranaki you can look back at the mountain. Surfing has an almost spiritual feel to it here. I'm in the sea every day, but it's still not enough.'

On any given day Daisy could be coaching or photographing her beloved sport, as well as actually surfing. She turns to look at the surf on Fitzroy Beach and exclaims, 'It's just there, just there!'

Easy Rider

Shaped by
Pete Anderson

Pete Anderson

In Search of the Green Board

The basis of surfing is about being at one with nature. It's about riding a wave of energy that, once ridden, can no longer be seen, with no record of it having ever been there. Except for the surfboards. Made mainly of polyurethane and coated in glass, they are far from eco-friendly and clash horribly with the ethos of the majority of surfers.

Highly sought after shaper and the person behind the famous 'ⓐ' logo, Pete Anderson is on a quest to create an environmentally sound surfboard, without compromising performance. His aim is to create a 100 per cent eco board that, at the end of the day, he can mulch up and put around his garden.

'Wooden boards don't work; they are never going to provide end performance. They go like pigs. It's about finding something that really works. If it's just eco-friendly and not great to ride, everyone will just put their blinkers back on and go back to their old boards.' Currently, high-performance boards are built using a polyurethane

foam core, covered in a non-recyclable piece of cloth and topped with three or four litres of polyester resin. It's a pretty toxic process.

Pete lives on a two-acre organic block in Opoutere, where he grows his own food and has been thinking about creating a 'green' board for a long time. He even gave money years ago to a student doing his master's degree on trying to find an eco-friendly core for the boards. At the moment he can build a 50 per cent eco board. It's made of a recyclable EPS foam (expanded foam), covered with a basalt cloth and topped off with a plant-based, solvent-free resin. The fins are made from recycled plastic. There's still a small glass component that is used to coat the board, so he would like to eliminate that.

There are also other people trying to create 'green' boards overseas. There's even a mushroom core that is 'grown', but it's too heavy. People rave about them but none is actually being ridden. Hemp has been used quite a bit, as well as bamboo and a few other materials.

This is Pete's second eco board and, as with the first, he's keen for his team riders to hammer them and let him know how he needs to improve them. 'I know this is far from perfect but I've got to start somewhere and this board is at least fifty per cent of the way there. It goes really well so I think the basis is really good.'

His infatuation with boards began when his sister bought one, and Pete and his brother Dave stole it from her. He loves the performance aspect of both the boards and surfing. On the water, he's always pushing his limits and seeing how hard he can perform. Even at 52 he claims he's still surfing pretty much like his younger self.

Seemingly at odds with his drive for performance, he also loves just chilling out on the water. 'I love sitting out there when it's quiet. I don't like the crowds that much any more, and the bar can get pretty busy. Luckily, I've been around long enough that I don't have to hassle for waves any more.' That's one of the attractions of living out at Opoutere — there aren't any crowds. Pete is often a lone figure on the water.

BOARDS
TO BE REPAIRED

Pete has been designing custom boards for over 30 years and the process is extensive. He gleans as much information from the rider as he can to get the best board for that person. How long have they surfed? Where are they surfing, and how often? What do they currently ride, and how does that board paddle? Apparently, the paddle bit is pretty important for a beginner or intermediate surfer. With the right board there's less energy expended paddling, which means more energy to catch all those waves.

The iconic Anderson motif was actually designed by a couple of surfer girls who were studying for an art degree. They had a bit of a play and asked if Pete liked the lower case 'a'. It's a bit like the '@' symbol, but modified. He's stuck with it because it's so recognisable.

'Every shaper is different but we are all artists in our own way. The machinery has changed shaping a lot but there's still plenty of room for the artistic side of things.' The boards have shortened up and widened, which Pete thinks is a good thing. For a while everyone followed Kelly Slater to a longer narrower board, but wider, shorter boards suit the shorter waves at his home break.

'It's really cool to have people like Ella Williams (see page 17) and my team guys riding my boards, as well as the young guys. I love hearing how they go.' Pete surfs alongside them so he can get immediate feedback on how his designs are working for them. He doesn't bother with written contracts for his team; it's all about loyalty and it's a two-way relationship. They all know he's working really hard to make great boards for them, and it's really important that his surfers provide him with honest feedback.

But at the end of the day, it'll only be when he's created a really great performance board that's also a 100 per cent eco board that he can mulch up and put around his garden, that he'll really be happy.

Jamie McDell

Singer/Songwriter/Surfer

As one of the country's most prolific songwriters, Jamie McDell has often been compared to Hawaiian acoustic guitar folk man Jack Johnson. And they both share a real love of the ocean and surfing.

'Surfing and songwriting are sort of the same thing for me. They are both just outlets for helping me get my head back in the play and giving me perspective on what I am doing. If I'm surfing a lot, then I do find it hard to write songs as I'm usually just really calm and happy with life. I don't have that much to say. When I'm working on a song, it feels so good to get it out there and say what I want to say. So both surfing and songwriting feel like a kind of therapy.'

Spending several years on a yacht in the Mediterranean as a seven-year-old introduced Jamie to the water, and she's enjoyed a love affair with it ever since. Currently on a 9-foot board but keen to get an older, longer classic board at some stage, Jamie loves surfing the long, slower waves on the East Coast.

Introduced to surfing by her best friend's father, Rod Smith, Jamie enjoys the simple things about surfing: getting out the back and just sitting there, chilling out for a while.

'I also love the learning side of surfing. I saw this guy who was just amazing and said to him, "You're so lucky to be able to do all those things on the board. I'm so jealous." And he just looked at me and said, "No. You're the one who's so lucky because this is the most fun learning experience you'll ever have. You only get to learn these things once. Now I know how to do it, it's not nearly as much fun. I don't get to have that buzz you get when you learn something new." It made me appreciate a whole different side to surfing. It reminded me that learning is fun.'

An ambassador for Surf Life Saving New Zealand for the past three years, Jamie is keen to use her influence with her 210,000-plus Facebook followers in a positive way. 'The main thing for me has been to be able to establish some kind of platform with my music, to encourage kids to want to get out on the water and be interested in the environment and conservation.'

'Surf life saving has given me heaps of confidence in the water and with surfing. I know it's not going to be that bad when I fall off. In New Zealand water anyway! No reef!'

She also loves the surf community and is out there every day during the summer. Her boyfriend also loves to surf so they often just head down to Pauanui for the day. 'It improves my whole week and changes my perception every time I go out so I think it's really worth it. For me it beats a night out, and I'm lucky I have loads of friends who also love surfing.'

Weaver

SURF BOARDS

Michael Thompson
— aka Mickey T

The Classic Longboarder

Halfway out to Manu Bay in Raglan, tucked away on the left-hand side of the road, is one of the most beautiful collections of designer boards you will find in New Zealand. Mickey T, as he is known to most, is usually busy hand-shaping boards while his lovely wife, Sunny, looks after the shop.

As a 19-year-old, with 'saltwater dripping from his nose', Mickey realised he didn't want to be dagging sheep for a living so got a job making Clark Foam blanks in Hamilton. But he didn't really think about making boards for a living until he went on a trip to the US, being fortunate enough to glass boards for a wide range of leading shapers in Hawaii — a massive learning experience. It was also during his time in America that he rode his first longboard, a Herbie Fletcher 8 ft 6 in, and he was hooked.

When he returned to New Zealand in 1991 the longboard revival was well under way and Billy Hamilton licensed Mickey to shape the Bear

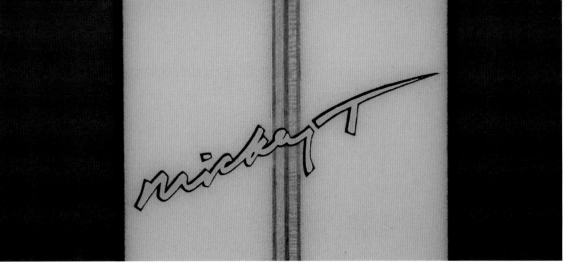

label, so he started producing longboards and Mini Mals. A few years on and Raglan Longboards was producing longboards, hybrids and classic surfboards. All the boards are crafted at their Raglan premises with attention to detail and using only the finest materials available. 'Our boards last ten to fifteen years, which in a way is probably not good business sense!'

Mickey speaks about the satisfaction he gets from people coming up to him and telling him how much they love the board he made them. 'It's one of the best things ... apart from surfing. I still really believe that if you want to get the most fun you can from surfing, then you need to speak to an experienced shaper and get a board that's right for you. We are all different and that's why we all need different surfboards.'

Mickey grew up a Raglan boy and started surfing at age 15 on a 6-foot Bob Davies single-fin.

'I was always kind of attracted to surfing, having seen it on TV, and I knew that Raglan had this awesome long left-hand break that everyone talked about so it was only natural that I got into it. I got hooked on it and ended up spending my life making surfboards. It's pretty dusty, dirty work if you don't love surfing.'

Still competing regularly and winning various age group events, Mickey's attitude is one of just not stopping. 'Nowadays, you keep surfing so you can keep surfing. I see the older guys who have stopped and, suddenly, they look completely different — they look like old men.'

At 58 he has a few years left in him before he'll think about taking up paddle boarding. He says, 'Old enough for the pension, old enough for the paddle. That's what I reckon, anyway.'

Mickey's approach to most things is pretty old-school and he loves the simplicity of surfing. 'Just you and your board, and off you go. There's all those hybrid sports — windsurfing, kite boarding, paddle boarding — but they all look complicated. None of them looks as pretty as surfing, to my mind.'

The majority of the time Mickey can be found riding one of his classic longboards, and, as much as he would love to still ride a short-board, it's just too crowded out there at Manu Bay. He's not interested in the claustrophobic feeling of sitting shoulder-to-shoulder with a bunch of guys.

Of all sports, it's surfing that has one of the longest learning curves, Mickey reckons. Especially learning with an adult body: it's totally different from how you learn as a kid and you're wasting your time on a short-board. But he thinks the happiest surfers out there are the beginners. 'Later on, you have your good days and your bad. But as a learner you love everything.'

Natalie Jacques

Wanderlust

The thought of starting a surf and yoga retreat was a concept that has always appealed to Natalie. Her background as a naturopath and yoga instructor, combined with her love of surf, natural medicine and adventure, all came together with the result being her dream business — Wanderlust.

Created for women in their twenties to thirties, Wanderlust is a female surf, yoga and wellness retreat based at Raglan, and is specifically designed for women who want to go on the ultimate surfing holiday and share it with other like-minded ladies. As well as being guided by Natalie to the best waves in Raglan, Wanderlust clients can also focus on the connection of mind and body through yoga in an ecologically sustainable, stunning natural environment. While Wanderlust is currently based at Raglan, there are long-term plans to take the retreats overseas.

Being able to provide retreats is a dream come true for Natalie. Having spent many years travelling the globe working — one job included being contracted by the Spanish government to spend six months on the Gold Coast investigating the surf industry — Natalie loves being based at one of the world's best, and also one of her favourite, surf spots.

'I believe in yoga so much and love combining it with surfing — they go so well together.' Natalie takes it one step further and believes this dedication should also be extended to the food you put in your mouth. It's a symbiotic balance.

Natalie has come a long way from the 14-year-old girl who felt a gravitational pull towards the ocean. She has a real love of being in the water and will go twice a day whenever she can. 'It's about being in the moment. It's the movement, it's the energy of the waves ... I would never choose to be in flat water.'

Jodie and Kirsty Vuletich

East and West

These identical twins embody everything that is great about surfing. They describe it as their 'addiction', and have made sure they have the best possible chance to surf every day by splitting up and living on both New Zealand's west and east coasts. Jodie lives at Baylys Beach on the west coast, while Kirsty lives at Mangawhai Heads on the east coast. Self-taught surfers who were given their first boards by their brother when they were 13, Kirsty and Jodie often drive the hour between the two points so they can surf together.

The twins share a cool tradition of collecting one shell off the beach after each surf they complete. They store them in a jar and then count them out each New Year's Eve.

Able to finish each other's sentences, the twins say there is little to tell them apart, other than that Kirsty was involved in a serious car

crash at age 17. She used surfing as a major motivation to quite literally get back on her feet. Not wanting her sister to get too much better than her while she was recovering from the accident was in itself great motivation, and, in the end, she only spent a year and a half out of the water. Still suffering from the side effects of a fractured spine and resulting nerve damage, Kirsty is unable to run or walk very far. But once on a board she is fine and the pain disappears. Any pain that reappears later is worth it for the surf.

Having both surfed overseas, they still each rate New Zealand surf as among the best they have ever experienced. So is east or west coast best? It would seem that west is best after all. Mainly because they can drive down to the beach and seek out their own little break.

'New Zealand has magic surf; it's got it all. It just rocks! Surfing keeps us young and alive. We feel sorry for people who don't surf.'

Surfing is their drug and they now understand what addiction is. This is the way they get high — even when the conditions are rubbish, even when they get smashed, it's worth it for that one good wave!

Mark Calcutt

'More than a lifestyle — it's a life.'

Reflecting on surfing, Mark realises how it has dictated his whole life.
Decisions like where to buy a house have been based around where
the best surfing beaches are. His vehicles have to be able to carry
particular boards, and holidays are booked around surf locations.
Surfing has influenced his clothing choices, and even his taste in music.
His watch is a tide model, and his dog is named 'Duke' after the famous
Hawaiian, Duke Kahanamoku (the father of modern surfing).

With so much of his life based around surfing, it's only natural that
Mark's artwork also reflects his love of the surf. His choice of medium
is a modern form of pastel and vivid watercolour, and he utilises its
pure palette as much as possible. Most of his artwork centres around
the ocean and waves, and when sitting out in the ever-changing water,
Mark is supplied with endless inspiration for his paintings.

Mark was instantly hooked after encountering his first open-faced wave at age 17, and he's been lucky enough to surf the full range of boards and even to work on boards (air-brushing surfboards at Breakwater Surf, County Line, Exit, and, recently, with his friend and neighbour, Denis Quane).

His wife and two daughters surf too. And his favourite place to surf is 'anywhere that's breaking nicely'.

As for so many in Christchurch, the earthquakes have had a profound effect on Mark, but the water has provided a wonderful distraction. 'It doesn't matter how stressed out you are or what's going on in your life, you leave it on the beach and for an hour or two you are somewhere else.'

Supersession

Thandi Tipene

A Champion Mother

Now that Thandi is a new mother, her newborn little girl has become her main focus and competitive surfing has taken a back seat. There will be three of them down on the beach in the near future, with the baby being swapped between Mum and Dad, depending on who is in the water; Dad is Bach Tipene (see page 136). Thandi says, 'I have noticed the few times I've been out lately that I've appreciated it a hell of a lot more than I did before. I'm probably even more conscious of things like what the rail is doing because I know I've only got a small window of time.'

Originally from Northland, Thandi remembers camping and surfing adventures with her own father at the beaches in their Hilux truck. 'Just me and Dad. Yeah, it was really cool. I had a six-foot single-fin orange fish.' She believes she was around 10 years old at the time. She used to swim competitively so she was pretty confident in the water.

She and Bach met at the beach through mutual friends, 'We said hi to each other and, I know it sounds bad, but as I was driving away with my friend I told him I was going to marry that guy.' He just laughed at

her, incredulous at her statement. Apparently, Bach had spoken about her to his friend, too. They bumped into each other a week later and have hung out together ever since, both on and off the water. They both understand each other's drive and love of the ocean.

Thandi has surfed all over the world. She and Bach lived across the road from Snapper Rocks in Australia for a year. They used to get up at 4 a.m. as the sun came up, and when the crowds were not so heavy, come in at 6 a.m. for pancakes, have a sleep, then go back out. 'It's such a good wave; one of my favourites, for sure, especially without the people.' The trip was part of their desire to progress as surfers, and to do it quickly they felt they needed to be where all the best surfers were.

They both worked part-time so they could get more time in the water, and were surfing alongside professional surfers such as Mick Fanning and Joel Parkinson, people she had looked up to and previously watched from afar. 'One time, Kelly Slater was out there. You just had to let it sink in. You don't want to surf badly, being among such world-class surfers every day; you make sure you're on top of your game.'

Thandi is also part of the team at CSA Surfboards. An accomplished surfer, she has won the New Zealand national title (2012), the New Zealand Maori nationals, and five or six consecutive Taranaki titles. 'It's great surfing here as it's a real community. I get nothing but respect from my fellow surfers. No one hustles me or anything like that.'

Thandi hasn't spent too much time in the water lately. Since her return, though, she has found her fellow surfers to be very chatty, asking about the new little one and seemingly giving her that extra bit of time and patience in the water, knowing she needs a bit of time to bring her surfing back up to her previous standard.

'I find surfing really grounding … definitely a spiritual experience. I reckon it's like a form of meditation. In life sometimes it's hard to be in the moment. While you're surfing, everything else slips into the background. You're on your wave, you're thinking about taking off, what turn you're going to do, so you're very present. When you're in the moment, you feel things more.'

Roger Hall

'Surfboards allow you to stand on water and ride waves — they are very special things.'

This leading board shaper has a very simple and practical approach to surfing: 'Some is better than none.' Ruakaka isn't a surfing mecca, but Roger has developed boards that don't require perfect waves. So it's all about just having fun. Roger stayed in Ruakaka because he didn't need anything else and didn't want anything else, and this simple approach to life carries across to his surfing. 'It doesn't matter what size wave it is, just get out there and have some fun.'

By the time Roger turned 25 he had been making surfboards for half his life and had just built his factory, which his company, Surfline, still works out of today.

Surfline makes between 200 and 250 surfboards a year — a relatively low number but it reflects the time spent individualising each board. From extensive consultation to custom-built stringers, the company's attention to detail and genuine love for the boards is first-rate. 'We start with polyurethane blanks, blown to a density which best suits the purpose of the end user. Then we custom glue with the appropriate timber stringers, glassing with polyester resins to a strength-to-weight ratio, which again speaks to the best interests of the end user.' The company's website proclaims: 'At Surfline, surfboards are cherished as objects of performance art, designed to give the best rides of your life, as well as the pleasure of owning a beautiful handcrafted surfboard.'

Roger's commitment to creating amazing boards also means, though, that he spends less time surfing than he used to, and his time on the water is now spent riding experimental boards, assessing what works and what doesn't. 'I'm still having a great time out there riding waves, but I know I'm thinking about it on a completely different level to everyone else.'

Roger doesn't believe in following the rules as a shaper and loves the challenge of designing different boards, currently designing finless boards. He hasn't ridden a board with fins for the past four years, and everything he rides now is 'way out of the box'. 'The direction boards themselves are heading in is so exciting. We have really only just scratched the surface with board design.'

Roger was approached by Barkers menswear to help the company create an authentic surfing clothes range to celebrate the history of surfing in the north, and Roger Hall's boards in particular. 'It was a real honour to be asked to collaborate with Barkers. They were keen to try to make their clothing line relevant, and it felt like massive recognition for my board shaping and involvement in the surf world. To be approached by people outside of surfers — that was really cool.' Roger's boards can also now be found for sale in the new Takapuna Barkers store, which has an authentic surf theme to it.

'Surfing is uplifting. It's exciting. The surfboard itself is the interface between you and the waves. Surfboards allow you to stand on water and ride waves — they are very special things.

'Surfing provides direction and focus. It's good for you physically, and it's good for you mentally. The ocean is an awesome place to play and it sets you up for a really good life. It's a great way to meet people and to explore your own country.'

It has been the best thing for Roger. 'I've got so much out of it. I just can't imagine not being a surfer, not to have surfing in my life.'

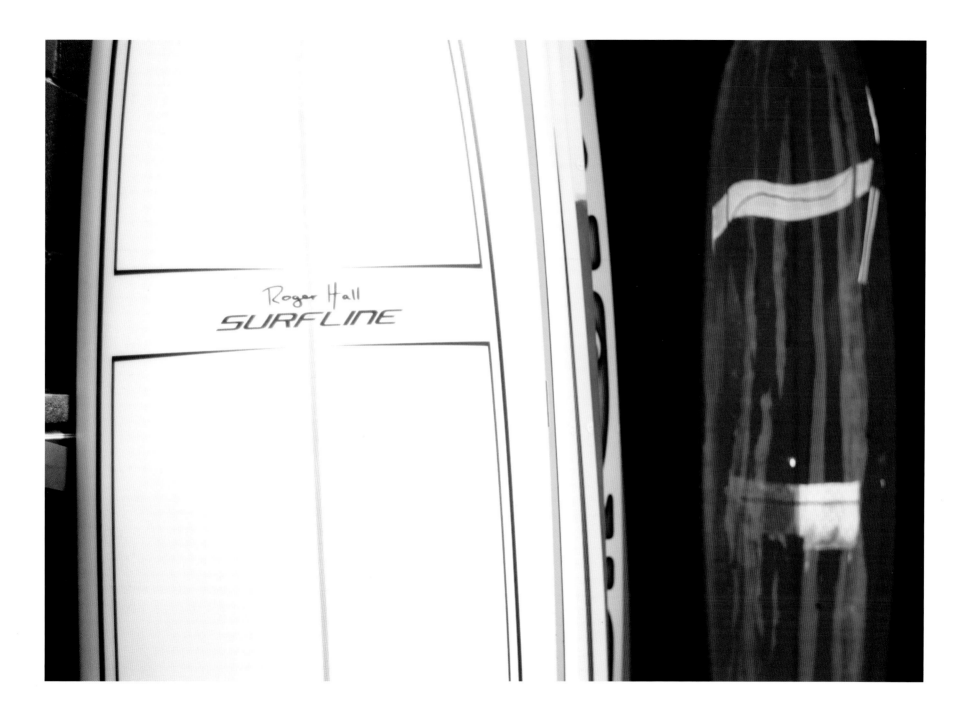

Roger Hall
SURFLINE

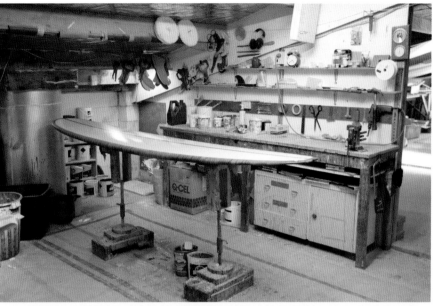

Surf Bettys

Party Waves

This is an example of social media site Facebook at its best: a community group set up for female surfers in the Auckland region who are looking for company to go surfing, or even simply for advice on the best spots, conditions and boards.

The name of the page derives from the world's most popular female board range, Surf Betty. Comprising proven NSP shapes and sturdy epoxy construction, the line-up is designed exclusively for girls. Experienced women surfers love the performance, while aspiring Surf Bettys are able to make progress on these user-friendly designs. Girl power, with no boys allowed!

The majority of female surfers don't start surfing until later in life. Unlike a lot of males who start in their teenage years or younger, women surfers often don't start until their twenties. They also don't have quite such a gung-ho attitude to the sport and don't want to travel miles on their own, nor are they keen to surf alone.

The owner of Ultimate Surf & Skate on Auckland's North Shore got tired of being asked the same questions all the time, so set up the Facebook page. It is now run by several members who help keep women updated on the best places, times and conditions to surf. Many of the members also use the page to touch base with other surfers and arrange times to meet and surf together. The page is also a really great place for foreigners and recent arrivals in New Zealand to meet other like-minded surfers.

Zarina Vazoeva

Thirty-one-year-old Zarina fell in love with surfing when she watched it on television back in her home country of Russia. There was a channel dedicated to extreme sports and it once showed someone riding a huge wave. 'I didn't even realise it was a popular sport – I just thought it was some genius!' Even though Zarina lived miles from the ocean, she thought it looked like something really cool to do. When she arrived in New Zealand and saw not only that lots of people surfed, but that she too could learn, she fell even more in love with the sport. She loved meeting so many great people and being able to travel to lots of beautiful places, following the waves.

Now Zarina looks at surfing differently. 'It's still "wow", but now I realise it's not just an extreme sport. It's more soulful; it's more about harmony and grace. It's like seeing different colours that you never knew existed. I will always remember that spark when I first saw it on TV — it was amazing.

'My first time surfing was at the Mount with two of my Russian friends, who I had convinced to come along with me. We were all screaming with excitement for the whole two hours. It was brilliant.'

Now that Zarina works full-time, surfing has to fit in around work hours so weekends are spent looking for waves. Omaha is her favourite place to surf because that's where she got her first green wave. 'I remember screaming and screaming when I saw it was green. It was only a small wave but I will never forget that amazing feeling of catching a green wave.

'My favourite thing about surfing is meeting people I would never have met otherwise and going to places I would never have gone. Having all those experiences like sitting on the beach, waiting for the sun to rise. For me, it's all about the soulful, romantic side of surfing. Like appreciating that the swell has travelled miles and miles just for me to ride it, to have this one little wave and this one moment of joy.'

Johanna Plata

Arriving in New Zealand in 2009, Jo thought that surfing looked like a lot of fun and wanted to give it a go. But her first lesson was awful and she ended up nearly drowning and being totally petrified. Determined that surfing was not going to defeat her, Jo overcame her fear of being in the water, and often under the water, with such a big object above her. She saw it as a huge challenge and one she's so pleased she overcame. 'I love surfing. Being in the ocean is amazing. I love the surfing community. They're all so friendly and you feel like you belong somewhere. My home is in Colombia so it's important for me to have the surf community here in New Zealand.'

Orewa is Jo's favourite spot to surf and she really appreciates the older surfers who are happy to chat and teach her things. 'I've learned so much from them in the water. They really look after me and I love it.'

Haidee Renata

'My dad took me out the back in Waipu when I was twelve. We both got up on the same wave and I still remember his huge smile and two thumbs up, cruising alongside me. It didn't last long because I freaked out with having him so close and stepped back on my board, causing it to fly up and smack me hard in the nose. I ended up being rushed to the surf club for some first aid and having a swollen nose for the next few weeks.'

Although Haidee started surfing when she was young, she didn't really take it up properly until she was in her twenties. A love of the ocean and spending time in the water with other people attracted her back to the sport.

A mum to an eight-year-old daughter who has already been surfing for two years, Haidee says surfing plays a huge part in her life. 'Surfing is now more than just a sport to me. It's a lifestyle. I have always loved the ocean and know that it's part of me. But it wasn't until I was an adult that I really came to appreciate the raw beauty of surfing and let it shape who I am.'

Usually a short-board rider, Haidee now also has a longboard so her daughter can surf on the front of it. Haidee's hope is that her daughter gets as much pleasure, love and respect for the ocean as she has.

'Just the simple joy of being away from everything when you are out on the water is awesome. No phones, no distractions; just you and the water, and maybe some dolphins! Life is normally so incredibly busy. Working in mental health, I'm often dealing with people's issues. It's so nice to get away from it all where it's just me, the water and the waves.'

Tony Baker

The Mangawhai Buddha

When Tony Baker starts talking about surfing, it's hard to get him to stop. Similarly, his involvement in the sport is all-encompassing. He's been a competitor, judge, team manager, coach, lifeguard, event organiser, and is now the chairman of the Mangawhai Board Riders Club.

He has also set up a surf school called Mangawhai Surf Dojo. When explaining the name, he says, 'To me, a dojo is a place of learning, and it involves every aspect of learning and education. I have been surfing since I was six years old and I am still amazed by the power and energy of the ocean each time I paddle out. There are so many lessons that can be learnt through our interactions with the beach, the ocean and the people associated with it.'

Mangawhai Surf Dojo is open to surfers aged five and upwards, and Tony's keen to share the pleasure he got from surfing at such a young age with other groms. 'I was approached last year by a group of keen parents wanting me to run ongoing, regular after-school surf coaching here in Mangawhai, and I have been so stoked with how it's gone.'

His father is a surfer, and he got Tony started on the waves. They moved to Mangawhai when he was 11 and on his first day surfing there he met a boy in the water and they've been friends ever since. That friend is now the president of the Mangawhai Board Riders Club and Tony the chairman. He grew up surfing whenever he could, and was lucky to end up going to New Plymouth Boys' High, which had a surf team. It wasn't great for his schooling but, ironically, he's now a teacher.

He started competing when he was a teenager although his transition into longboarding, aged 17, wasn't the smoothest. An argument with his dad resulted in his short-board being snapped in half — later replaced with a beautiful Bear LB. He now owns a wicked quiver of boards currently numbering 16. Mangawhai is a perfect spot for longboarding and Tony has also competed all over the world. 'I've got friends from all over the country from surfing. The competition side of surfing is so cool — I love to win but I also love the community side of things and everyone getting together. Surfing has allowed me to travel, meet loads of people and has given me so many opportunities.'

Tony is well-known among the local and national surfing community, having had a successful competitive career on the New Zealand longboard circuit, as well as competing in regional and international events on both short-board and longboard. He is also a senior lifeguard at Mangawhai Heads.

Over the past five years Baker has also been a selector, coach and team manager for the New Zealand junior surfing team, along with coaching and managing Northland surfing teams. 'In 2012 and 2013, I was lucky enough to be selected as the manager of the New Zealand surfing team so I got to go to Panama and Nicaragua. Working with elite surfers was amazing. I was so proud to go and represent the country, even though I wasn't competing myself. There's just so much good stuff that has come out of surfing for me.'

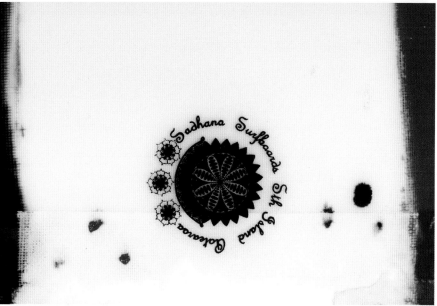

Gary McCormick

'Surfing was the making of me.'

Not many people know that Gary McCormick spent 16 years cleaning toilets at a girls' school. After dropping out of law school and following the call of the waves to Gisborne, Gary took up the job for one reason: so he could go surfing every day.

Titahi Bay, Porirua, was a fairly grim, working-class neighbourhood, which, to put it mildly, was an intimidating environment for a middle-class teenage boy to grow up in. Not being particularly good at sports and finding very little 'street cred' in reading books, the discovery of surfing and a polystyrene board opened up a whole new world for Gary.

An older boy at school who surfed, Dave Timbs, became his hero. Older brothers and their boards provided a confidence that had been lacking in the fairly hostile environment he was growing up in. Surfing sans wetsuits and in old rugby jerseys in howling Wellington southerlies gave Gary a physical outlet, which evolved into the '60s hippie surfing culture, a lifestyle of long hair, dope-smoking and alternative culture.

When surfing started out in New Zealand, surfers were like the Hells Angels. People use to look down on them; there was a real dislike of the surfing culture, and yet now it's a mainstream sport. It suited

Gary's personality when it was an outsider's sport, as he had never thought of himself as a popular culture person. 'I'm really glad I was there in the early days. Everyone who was out on the water in those days was a real character, otherwise they would have been holding down a full-time job in an office.'

While still at high school in Titahi Bay, Gary sold boards for DEL Surfboards, which was a great way to try out all the good, and bad, boards that were being produced.

Dave Timbs moved up to Gisborne — in those days the California of the South Pacific — and so Gary followed. There he stayed for 16 years, cleaning toilets at Central School every afternoon, and surfing every morning.

A chance meeting with a documentary film-maker resulted in Gary being hired as a researcher in Raglan. The end result was an award-winning documentary, *Raglan by the Sea*, which then evolved into the Heartland TV series and thus Gary's beginnings in the media. It was the perfect transition from surfing into the media, with many stints spent filming followed by time surfing.

'What initially drew me to surfing was the pure romance to begin with, just the ridiculous idea of standing up on a plank and riding on a wave. Then surfing drove me into reading counter-culture material and Cultural Revolution ideas. The lovely 'sixties Cultural Revolution introduced me to poetry, and I always thought of surfing as a poetic existence. (Subsequently, Gary ended up writing poetry, had several books published, and toured with Sam Hunt.)

'The spiritual element of surfing really captivated me. It's a form of dance and, done well, it's a very gracious pastime. It transcends other things. You can find yourself on an isolated beach, paddling out as the sun rises. It's an experience that is unique. There are very few other sports that combine nature, beauty, environment, weather and your own spiritual outlook.'

These days, you won't find Gary out on the water. Split Enz member Noel Crombie once said, 'Surfing was during my outdoor period', and that's how Gary feels. He could go out there and flounder around, but he's too much of a perfectionist to do surfing half-heartedly. 'Wisdom means you decide to do what you do when you can do it well. I don't like doing things I can't do well.

'Surfing has a tipping point where it becomes so profound, almost like a religious experience, that it actually alters your whole set of values. It certainly did for me. I took it up because I wanted to be good at something, but then it altered my whole sense of values. Surfing is what made me. If you are a fucked up person, you cannot surf — you have to have that inner quiet.'

Daniel Farr

Taranaki Grommet

Talking with Daniel Farr, you quickly realise that he's a modest, well-mannered 15-year-old athlete with lofty aspirations. He says he managed to win the Rip Curl GromSearch 2014 competition because the top seed was knocked out in the semis, 'so that made it a bit easier'. One of the other local guys, Isaac Kettle, was leading for the majority of the 25-minute final of the U17 Boys division. On his last wave, Daniel scored a six, which pushed him into first position. Five seconds to go and he took off on a wave with Isaac just after him, both hunting for the winning score. Daniel was forced to exit the wave but he had stood up first, which meant that Kettle incurred an interference. Daniel held on to win.

His face lights up as he tells me. 'I was stoked to win it because there was a trip up for grabs to compete in the international GromSearch final in Indonesia. The top boy and girl from eight regions got to go to Lakey Peak, Dompu. Surfing with guys like Jakey [Jacob] Willcox

and Pat Curren was so cool, watching how they surfed those conditions. If I'm going to pursue this as my career, I need to learn to surf as well as those guys.' An incredibly modest description when you consider this worldwide series selects the top eight male and eight female surfers to represent their country at this prestigious event.

He is currently rated as the top in his age group in the New Zealand U17 rankings. There are six competitions around the country, held at places such as Piha, Whangamata and Tauranga. At each event there are points to be earned depending on where you place in that competition. Simply put, the person with the most points wins the series and the title. Within that national race is the Billabong series, three out of the six events. He won the Billabong title last year and this year.

'There's a bit of pressure and I do get a little nervous, but before each comp I try not to think about the past, just focus on every heat, just trying to win the next comp.'

His mum, Shelley, says he must have been four or five when he first surfed. Daniel doesn't remember. Originally from South Africa, the Farrs moved to New Zealand when Daniel was five. His first memory of surfing was with the Taranaki Christian Surfers group. Dad David got involved with them and took Daniel to learn to surf every Saturday morning. 'I just remember going along to that and having fun in the shore break on a really long old board.'

What does he look for in a board now? 'How it goes in the water, the lines that it draws. A longboard would have longer drawn out lines, but the boards I ride, short-boards, stay tighter in the pocket and do the sharper turns. I like something that will float and draw the lines well and something that will get me straight up and down onto the lip of the wave. I'm still trying to work on my airs but it's pretty hard, especially the landing.'

David is probably the biggest influence in Daniel's surf quest. David surfed in South Africa from the age of 12. He rode every day for an hour or so after school, and lived directly opposite a hospital, which Shelley says he needed to visit quite often. Once he got stitched, he would go straight back out to surf.

Shelley and David have three children: Josh (almost 17), Daniel (15), and Rebecca (13). All of them surf and all of them are home schooled. Surfing wasn't the main consideration but it has definitely benefited. Shelley explains, 'When they were first learning to surf and if the conditions were right, we could just pack up and head to the beach.' As they got better, Shelly did get frustrated at times, knowing how much schoolwork was sitting at home when the waves were good. 'But we worked out a good balance in the end, I think.'

When it's competition time, surfing probably comes first, and school second. Non-competition time and schooling definitely goes back to being first priority. 'We set goals, and once those goals are achieved then they can head back to the surf.' It would seem that Daniel is really good at this. 'He's focused and he just gets on and does what he needs to do.' Taranaki has a fairly large home school community, comprising over 60 families. 'All have different reasons for home schooling — I think that's what makes the group so good. Diversity.' The unifying passion of the parents is the children: educating them and spending time with them.

One overriding lesson that surfing has taught Daniel is patience. It's a rare virtue in our modern society. 'Waiting for the right wave, just trying to find the best wave to be able to do the best turns on, is all about patience. One wave at a time, one heat at a time, that's the way to surf to the best of my ability.' Daniel's advice to someone just starting to surf is about perseverance. 'You'll get smashed a couple of times, but you'll get there. Just keep going.'

When asked what his favourite thing about surfing is, he comes back with a short, simple reply: 'Getting barrelled, being in the tube and looking out.' He pauses and seems to go somewhere else for just the briefest of moments, and adds, 'Time slows down in there.'

Mike Yukich

The Historian

You would be hard-pressed to find a more dedicated surf enthusiast than Mike Yukich. Described by his peers as a surfing bachelor, Mike definitely leads a life that has surfing at the core of it. He collects old surfboards, archives surf magazines, and loves nothing better than travelling overseas to compete in surf meets and attend surfboard auctions.

'I consider myself to be an archivist more than a collector. For me, history is more important than nostalgia.' His archive starts from 1961. He has almost all of the surf magazines from Australia, the US and New Zealand that were published during the 1960s and '70s. People would leave boxes of old magazines on his back doorstep and there is an international network of collectors that help each other, plus there are online auctions. 'I still subscribe to *Surfer* magazine, *The Surfer's Journal*, and I get every issue of *New Zealand Surfing Magazine*.'

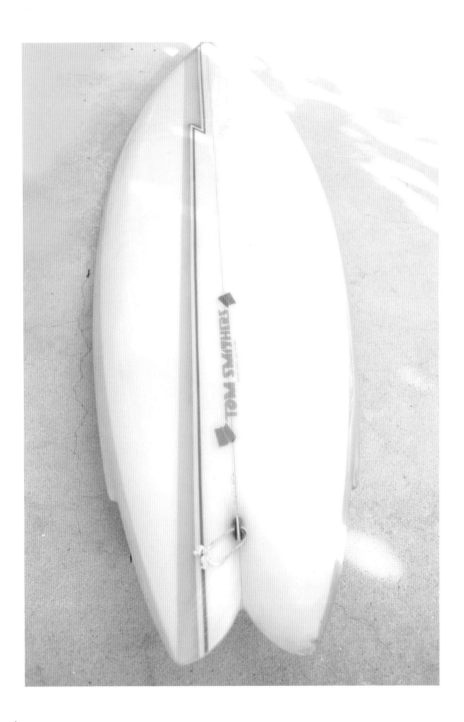

With a real joy for swapping surfing stories, Mike not only loves surfing but also gets real enjoyment from meeting and getting to know other surfers. 'Surfers are generally adventurous types and they can be trendsetters as well. At the surf comps, just being able to watch a certain standard of surf riding, and catching up with other surfers — it's all quite inspiring.'

It's hard to quantify how much surfing has affected his life choices. Job opportunities just happened to turn up in surf areas, allowing Mike's love affair with the waves to flourish.

Just back from Byron Bay in Australia and heading to Hawaii for another competition later in the year, Mike was up front with his bosses at work. A project engineer with Gisborne City Council, Mike is glad the bosses understand his need to spend time on the water. The job is still being done but work hours are flexible around his surfing time. The values that have come from surfing have encroached into other areas of his life. He mostly works on water supply projects, and particularly enjoys it if he can have a direct effect on the water quality of the ocean he so loves to surf. He was employed as a project engineer for a new wastewater treatment plant that was completed in 2011. 'I was really drawn to this job as I saw it as an opportunity to make a significant difference to the inshore environment where I was surfing.'

Mike started surfing on a rubber mat at Piha when he was 10, graduating to a stand-up board when he was 13. Now an avid surfboard collector, he currently has around 30 boards. The spare room is cluttered with them and they provide the added bonus of being a great talking point. He loves buying surfboards off Trade Me, but it's even better if he can rescue local boards, as he loves to hear the stories and the history behind them.

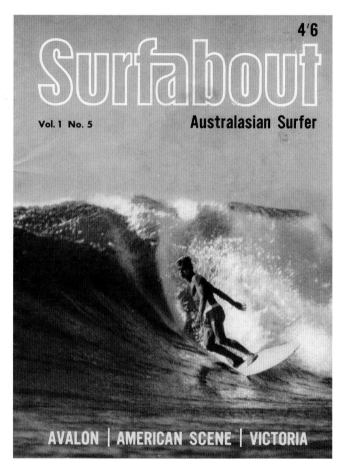

Wendy Andrews

A Family that Plays Together Stays Together

Wendy loves her longboard and you can see why. It's simply beautiful, inlaid with a piece of floral material that's reminiscent of the traditional Hawaiian image of longboarding. It's even more precious since she sourced the material herself, and had the board designed by Denis Quane, and completed by Sadhana Surfboards of Christchurch. It's one of a kind.

Like many female surfers, Wendy began surfing in her twenties so she could spend more time with her husband. A national age group surfer, husband Steve surfs most days, and now the passion has become a real centre point for the whole family. Their eight-year-old son Johnny is also learning to surf and is being taught by local instructor Aaron, who previously taught Wendy.

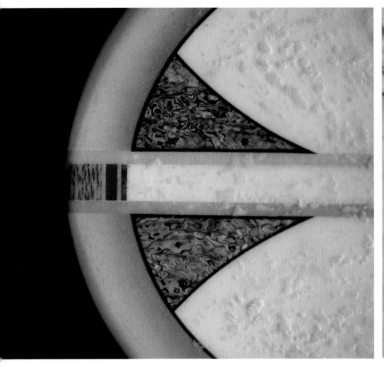

'We love any time near the ocean and spend all our time on the beach. We are members of the Sumner Longboard Club. There are fifty-odd members and they are really our community, or family. It's who we spend all our time with. There're loads of families and it's an awesome club — really good people.'

Surfing for Wendy is all about just having time at the beach. Having a surf sets her up for another week of work, and recharges her batteries. Stand-up paddle boards (SUPs) are now part of Wendy's quiver and, as she heads into her mid-forties, she's found that SUPing is so much kinder on her back.

'Our whole family is now into it. We go over to Noosa every winter and get to surf there in amazing conditions. No wetsuits makes a great change from Sumner, which is pretty much wetsuits all year round. But in the middle of winter it's still awesome conditions here — really calm, cold and no crowds.'

Wendy and Steve's garage is lined with boards, including a beautiful Roger Hall classic longboard, which is Steve's pride and joy. It has paua inlaid throughout the board and is completed with a paua fin. Surfboards definitely take priority over cars in this garage.

the
SUMO
by McTavish

RAGLAN LONGBOARDS
SHAPES BY MICKEY T
NZ

David Timbs

Saltwater Therapy

'Surfers are not the dropouts that society has often believed them to be. They are the "go aheads". They understand the meaning of being in the now. They know there is nothing left after you have ridden the wave. It's gone — you don't leave a trail. It's not like making a painting or writing a song. When you are finished riding the wave, there is no proof you were ever there. Very zen.'

David Timbs is obviously a man very in tune with both the world around him and his own thoughts. The runt of the family with an older brother who surfed, David grew up in Titahi Bay, learning to surf on flat wooden belly boards. He can't remember when he started surfing; he was just always in the water, playing on the waves. Maybe it was growing up in a house on the beach, but standing up on a board just felt like the most natural thing in the world to him. With his mates, including Gary McCormick (see page 92), David would spend hours sitting around talking about what you could do on a board. How you could move around on it, make the board itself turn, and, naturally, how you could make the board go faster. There was no internet or even magazines to learn from and so they taught themselves.

'When you have an experience like that at a young age — going surfing without a wetsuit in the middle of winter at Titahi Bay — well, something's driving you. You know you had a good experience once; you don't necessarily know what it was, but you want to repeat it. That's the drug.'

That feeling of having had an experience but not being able to define it sent David on a lifetime search. Intrigued by the euphoria that surfing brought him and the way the saltwater could change his state, David spent many years studying various meditative practices. 'Surfers over the years have looked for a similar experience off the water, often with music and drugs, seeking that same feeling — looking for it over and over. It's such a spiritual feeling that it's hard to describe.'

Experiencing other realities without using drugs, and learning about various Eastern practices, made him realise that repeating the surfing experience is the closest thing to it. That non-thinking state, which he describes as the 'space between the thoughts', is what happens when you are surfing. 'Because everything is happening so quickly when you are trying to catch a wave. You have a moving medium in the wave, the surfboard, the wind and everything else. You don't have time to think so it becomes a reflex, a non-thinking state. But in the time leading up to it you are thinking quite intensely. Choosing where to sit, which wave to take, when to paddle into the wave. All those things take a lot of thought, but then, all of a sudden, you have this non-thinking experience. You can't recall it later so it is non-thinking. And I think that's what gets people addicted.'

Something else that had a profound effect on David was a near-death experience as a 23-year-old. He was sailing on a trimaran from New Zealand to Tonga when the yacht was caught in a cyclone 700 miles offshore. Lucky to be back on dry land and realising that he had survived, Dave discovered a new philosophy: What's the worst that can happen? You can die! Ever since, he has always tried to follow his desires rather than fear the outcome of his decisions. 'At least I've got a pulse' is the mantra he's lived by most of his life.

A job opportunity saw David move to Gisborne 40 years ago, and the world-class surf breaks have kept him there ever since. 'I guess we keep repeating what we are successful at in life.'

Chris Watson

In Possession of the Magic Board

The sight of this self-confessed computer geek riding his ex-postie's motorbike through Raglan, complete with cut-down windsurfing board attached, is enough to make anyone smile.

Chris's story is as unique as his approach to surfing, and he is as far removed from the high-end professional surfers that grace our television screens as you can possibly get.

He began surfing in Middleborough, northeast England, in 6 ml neoprene in freezing conditions. After travelling the world, Chris ended up in New Zealand, tiki-toured around the country and, during a visit to Raglan, fell completely in love with it. (Interesting, then, that his favourite place to surf is Spot X, just south of Christchurch …)

Chris has since bought two acres of cow paddocks in Raglan that were a failed subdivision, planted a few thousand trees, and put up a tiny cabin that he lives in. He works remotely, tapping keys — otherwise known as being a 'project and business analyst' — mostly for IT companies in the US. The majority of his clients think he's working in the States too, and Chris doesn't worry too much about correcting them. It means he can spend half his days surfing, or riding around Raglan on his bike.

The board currently attached to the bike was shaped by a local legend called Gregor. 'He lives out at Whale Bay in an amazing house that he's hodgepodged together over the past twenty-five years. I have lived in his sleep-out (called the Bat Cave) for a few winters.' Gregor cut the surfboard down from a windsurfing board that he pulled apart, and it even has a bit of glitter in the glass job. The cork tile he added to the tail is his way of fine-tuning the board's performance — no need to wait for the glass to dry. It's known all around Raglan as 'the magic board', and has been ridden by the many people who have stayed with Gregor over the years.

If the conditions are right, Chris surfs every day. It's not about being an amazing surfer or catching the biggest waves. It's about everything else that makes up surfing as an experience.

'I love all the stuff on the periphery, really. I think the bit of going down a wave and standing on a board is just a few seconds of the whole thing. It's all the other stuff. It's the first duck-dive in the morning when you get the spray reflecting off the sunlight. It's the trips with your friends, the companionship. It's the anticipation of surfing.'

Donna Henderson

Surf Coach

A borrowed wetsuit and surfboard at age 25 hooked Donna and changed her life. Getting a job with surf brand Roxy also fuelled the fire and began her love of teaching people to surf. Fifteen years of surfing later and Donna is a fully qualified surf instructor and founder of the Christchurch School of Surf.

People often tell Donna that she is living the dream, and she usually has to agree. Living at Taylors Mistake, and with her school based at Head Street, Scarborough (it has a long, slow, undulating wave, which is perfect for longboarders or beginners), Donna can give a few lessons and still fit in a surf every day. A big advocate for getting women into surfing, she used to help run the Roxy Surf Jams, which introduced thousands of girls to surfing. She has created 'Learn to Surf' days for women, which provide a perfect chance to try out surfing in a safe, friendly and positive environment.

Donna has also added a new surf session this summer in the form of a social surfing group for women each Thursday morning. The group is a real mix of women — most have their own boards and wetsuits but don't have anyone to surf with. Through Facebook, Donna updates everyone and provides a time and place to meet, surf and have a laugh together. The camaraderie of surfing with other women is a real drawcard and keeps them coming back each week.

Donna was back surfing two days after the birth of her first child and she now loves surfing with her children, in particular nine-year-old Ava. Being able to share her passion with her daughter is something very special. Donna believes that repetition is the key to surfing. 'The more time you spend in the water, the better you get — and if you're not in the water, you're not going to get any better.'

Her love of teaching people to surf is contagious. 'I just get such a buzz out of surf coaching. It's a pretty easy skill to teach and to pick up. Anyone can surf, even children who have been told they are no good at all sorts of other things. It's great to see those kids in particular get a buzz out of catching a wave. That feeling of accomplishing something that they see the pros doing on TV, accompanied by the "buzz" that comes with actually catching a wave — that's gold. At the end of the day, everyone is smiling.'

Shaped by
Pete Anderson

Janine and Dean Williams

Saltwater in Their Veins

It's taken a few years but the extended Williams family has now accepted that for Dean, Janine and their two children, Christmas Day is all about surfing. 'They now know that it's always got to be Christmas dinner [not lunch], it's got to be late, and, yes, we will be the last there,' laughs Janine. 'Being able to spend Christmas Day together — just the four of us out on the water — is very special. It's such a great day as it's our one day all year which is totally dedicated to family surfing. Nobody has to work, nobody has any commitments, and we can all hang together.'

The Williams family is an example of the joy that can come from a whole family sharing the love of surfing. What started off as a hobby for Dean and Janine has taken over all their lives — and in the most positive of ways. They now own and run the Whangamata Surf Shop,

where they can be found if they are not either out surfing or travelling the world with their daughter Ella, pro surfer and 2013 World Junior Champion (see page 17).

'Ella's been surfing since she was four,' says Dean. 'I used to tuck her inside my wetsuit and paddle out to catch waves. She'd sit on the front of the board, then start trying to pull herself up. She would grab on to my hair and hold on. Since then she's been unstoppable.'

Dean and Janine have both been around surfing since before they can remember and the whole family seems to have saltwater in their veins. Son Braedon, who is a few years older than Ella, is just as besotted with surfing as the rest of his family. Both the kids started surfing at Raglan when they were about four years old.

Dean, a panel beater by trade, has been surfing for 44 years. When he starts talking about surfing, his whole manner changes. 'There's just nothing that beats being out there on the bar. It's different every time, unlike in a skateboard bowl. The surf changes with the wind. It's always a combination of swell *and* wind, and therefore it's always different.'

It's 14 years since the family sold up everything and moved across from Hamilton to Whangamata. The Surf Shop itself has over 40 years of history and is the oldest surf shop in the area. It needed an injection of new energy and fresh enthusiasm, something the whole family has in abundance.

As Dean says, they are heading in the same direction and all sharing the same passion. 'There are not many families that can say that, and we are just lucky that they both (Ella and Braedon) chose surfing because they were both also very good at other sports. Having the whole family in the water is just the best. Even Ella made it before dark last night so we all managed one wave together, which is just a great feeling. We have fifty or sixty boards at the house. It's crazy. But there's something there for every occasion. You can't just have one board — every day is so different.'

Janine considers herself a 4-foot wave rider, as the bigger waves bring out all the hotshot surfers. It changes the whole vibe out on the bar and Janine is only out there to have fun. But she catches her fair share of waves, and hearing her talk about her latest board illustrates her love of the sport. 'It's a Chilli Rare Bird five-foot ten-inch — I love it! I saw a girl walking down the beach in Portugal holding one, and as soon as I got home I started trying to track one down. I've surfed on it for fourteen days straight and I'm buzzing like a kid with a new toy. I just knew the board was going to be the one.'

There are quite a few surfing families in Whangamata, and the bar is a very competitive wave. 'Having that on our back doorstep is pretty choice. It's always great when friends are catching waves, but when it's your own family it's even better — we're always whooping and yelling, having a great time.'

Matt King

Old-school Surfing

Meeting Matt King is like jumping back to the '60s and meeting an old-style surfer, complete with beard and a love of retro boards. He is a gentle, mellow character who obviously gets so much enjoyment out of the simple beauty of surfing. Growing up in a surf-mad family (apart from his mum, who's petrified of the water), Matt knew there was a high chance he'd become a surfer. But he's not just a guy who surfs; he's someone who embodies all the traditional elements of surfing longboards. Even off the water, he moves with the calmness and grace required to skilfully manoeuvre such a large bit of foam. His appreciation for the traditions and the old art form of board riding is contagious.

He talks about the joy of surfing with his dad and brother and now his partner, and how nothing beats hanging out on the water with them. Childhood holidays were spent at a bach at Ruakaka, and there are even photos of Matt on a surfboard at about the age of three.

These days, his parents' garage in Whangamata often has no space to park cars as, between them, they would have in excess of 40 boards.

Surfing has influenced so much of Matt's life. He went to New Plymouth as a student because of the waves, and now works for O'Neill surf clothing company.

Like many, he started on short-boards, but followed his brother, accomplished surfer Ian, onto the longboards when it wasn't considered the thing to be riding. DEL surfboards are what he likes to ride. Matt reckons that since they've been making them in New Plymouth since 1965, it must mean they know what they're doing. Old-style boards are what Matt and his family are into, with a real appreciation for the '60s style of graceful nose riding and turning with full control. It's all about making the difficult look easy, as opposed to a lot of the modern longboards, which often result in surfers making the easy look difficult!

A real purist, Matt's not really keen on the competition side of things. They're about forcing things rather than flowing with the wave, he reckons. He worries that people who compete often spend their downtime on the waves practising moves that will score well in competitions, rather than chilling out and enjoying the moment.

For Matt, surfing is about being able to focus on something to improve, and hanging with like-minded people. Being in the water with dolphins and whales makes for very special times. Plus there's the added bonus of the fit and healthy lifestyle. Essentially, he cannot think of anything else he'd rather be doing.

Wayne 'Arch' Arthur

On the Airwaves

Most Fridays between 4 and 5 p.m., Arch can be found in the cosy studio of Taranaki's The Most 100.4 FM radio station as co-host of the *Out the Back Surf Show*. Previously a student radio station, The Most uses the segment to take an irreverent look at surf culture, or, as they put it, 'News, views, and who's dropping in on who'.

Arch is a warm, sociable, larger-than-life character, who quickly puts people at ease. He is also the founder of the current New Plymouth Surf Riders Club. The previous clubs fell by the wayside for a variety of reasons, including surfers not being responsible enough to have any longevity past the compulsory 6 o'clock pub closing. The club's current membership is made up of all the old guys who used to be in the earlier clubs. They formed a constitution and a few objectives to figure out where they were headed, one objective being to get a New Zealand champion in the region again. Taranaki had been a surfing powerhouse in the past.

Arch claims they were damned lucky to score the clubhouse premises they now have on Fitzroy Beach. It was destined to be. While walking home after 6 o'clock one evening, Arch spotted the building and thought it could be a great little clubhouse. He discovered the council was in the middle of granting the lease to another body. On Sunday, a meeting was called for Tuesday, and 61 guys turned up with $100 each, and they formed the surf club, informed the council that they were a proper club with $6000 in the bank and the wisdom of two previous failed attempts under their belt. The Taranaki surfer 'rowdy rebel' image was becoming somewhat tarnished as a few of them had become ratepayers and gained senior positions in the community, and so the slow slide to respectability began.

Arch's first experience of surf was in 1962, watching people at an inner-city beach in New Plymouth while he was still a snotty-nosed little grommet. Surfboards were a fairly hard item to get hold of back then so a little experimentation ensued. While down at Ngamotu Beach at the fishing and diving shed, he came across his father's water ski, and so attempted a bit of body surfing on it, quite successfully. This led to Arch and a mate having a go at making a surfboard in the garden shed. They took it over to Back Beach, where it lasted about four waves before it broke in half. But just being on those few waves was enough to grab Arch. His sister, who was working at the time, lent him the money to buy a second-hand board.

Other sports Arch tried included underwater fishing and scuba diving (back when aqualungs, a twin-hose underwater breathing apparatus, was used), and his heroes were people like Hans Hass and Jacques Cousteau, the legendary French marine explorer. Arch was severely asthmatic as a kid and in running races at school he would place last. The family doctor suggested literally throwing him in at the deep end and getting him in the water. Arch proved to be reasonably good at swimming and went on to try skin-diving and snorkelling, and then aqualunging. The idea was to use the water for different things in different conditions, something to do on the rough and the calm days. But even on the calm days, they managed to find surf in Taranaki.

Right at the beginning, Arch and his friends explored the whole New Plymouth coast and found all the spots. As the price of petrol went up, access to transport became less reliable. If he had to pick his favourite place to surf, it would be the Awakino river mouth, Fitzroy and Back Beach.

Recently, Arch wanted to impress some friends he had staying from Hawaii because, well, Hawaii is such a great place. He tried to cram heaps of activities into their trip to Taranaki, taking them to the bach, gathering paua and crayfish, a little fishing and even a little surf. 'It was amazing to hear them say: "Oh, you lucky bastards!", "Imagine living here", "It doesn't get any better than this", as they were sitting on the deck, eating great Kiwi food and watching the surf.'

What a wonderful example of the Surf Riders' motto: *Come as a guest, leave as a friend.*

Roger Hall
SURFLINE

Bach Tipene

Sponsored Rider,
Team CSA Surfboards

Bach's father and brother both surfed so it was a given that he was going to walk from the black iron sands of Ohawe Beach and take to the water. He learned the basics of his surf skills until he was around 11 in and around Hawera. Then his family moved and the Patea river mouth became his local break, a much more dangerous place to learn.

There are two piers either side of the river mouth, which used to be the New Plymouth port. 'I learnt to surf up the river. On the outside of the river the wave was big, like six to seven foot, but it would reduce in size as it travelled up the river. So you could choose where you wanted to go in.'

The river provided a natural progression for a brave young grom, moving to the bigger, outside waves as courage and ability grew, and slowly working up the nerve to go to the outsides of the piers. This was Bach's playground until he was 18 when his parents moved again, this time to New Plymouth and a new home break of Back Beach. It has fast short rides, and, if the sand is in the right spot, you can get a longer surf. Bach believes it's the most consistent spot in New Plymouth.

No one else surfed at his high school so he was pretty much a loner at the start. That is until everyone caught on to the fact that it was a fun sport. 'It was good for me. I preferred being in the ocean to playing touch rugby after school. Once everyone got into surfing there was a core group of us.'

As a kid he just wanted to be sponsored. He didn't really think much further than that. Seasons Surfboards sponsored him when he was around 15, and also sponsored his older brother. Now he's with Cain Aldridge (see page 145) at CSA Surfboards. 'I think I was his first team rider.'

Bach stopped surfing at one stage for a period of time; he was jaded by surf competitions. 'It's pretty tough when you're not winning. It was draining and took away the fun.' So he stopped surfing completely and went snowboarding instead. 'I came back eventually when I realised how much fun it really is. There are not many sports, if any, that can compete with surfing … the skill and the intuition of reading the ocean. It's a hard thing to master.'

Bali, Indonesia, Samoa, Tahiti, France, Spain, South Panama, North and South America are places where Bach has been lucky enough to surf. Sometimes it was to compete, like with the New Zealand surf team in Panama and Tahiti, sometimes a surf trip.

He was the Men's National Champion 2013 (Over 28s), and also Maori National Champion (2010). 'It was a great milestone for me, especially as I had been away from surfing for the four years previously. I really enjoyed the comp. I've seen old illustrations of Maori surfing on wooden plank boards. Obviously, the ocean is really important in our culture, being a big provider of kai moana.'

Where to next for Bach Tipene? 'I'm just doing it for me, for the love of surfing. That's the way I'll stay happy. Sometimes it's the smallest thing that can make it worthwhile.' The internet means that now surfers can see what other surfers are up to. 'Sometimes you can get fixated on being able to do progressive new moves rather than trying to improve your own skills. When I surf I put all my energy into it. The simplest things in surfing can sometimes give you the most rewards. Even getting barrelled.' Maybe he is more of a master than he is letting on, given that the barrel is the ultimate pinnacle for many surfers.

'Being in a barrel is almost like time travel — it slows time down — it's real crazy. As the water curls over the top of you, every microsecond counts.'

Ambrose McNeill

Intrepid Surfer

The pain of broken bones from skateboarding was what led 24-year-old Ambrose to try surfing, and once he got out there and experienced his first 'dream wave', he realised that not only was this cool but this was him. Drawn to the open environment and being surrounded by nature rather than concrete, Ambrose loved that with forever-changing waves, 'you're never going to get the same wave twice'.

From a family of nomads, Ambrose says it's been the most natural thing to follow the waves. Qualifying as a surf instructor gave him a 'ticket to travel', and, after emailing every surf school he could find on the internet, he got his first job in France.

A Bachelor in Sports Coaching from Canterbury University, followed up by a post-grad teaching diploma, means he has a qualification to fall back on. In the meantime, following summer around the globe is his priority, but 'travelling with a purpose' is how he describes it. Surfing provides connections with people, even when

you don't speak the same language, and this has allowed Ambrose to make bonds with people he would never have met visiting monuments.

Even though Ambrose has surfed all around the world, for him there's nothing quite like surfing at home in Sumner, Christchurch. Paddling out with a bunch of friends, knowing everyone in the line-up and having a really good laugh, is for Ambrose what it's all about.

His favourite board is a Sadhana by Jay Jackman, a 9 ft 6 in single-fin; Ambrose had it custom-made to reflect the cover of his musical father's first album. Malcolm McNeill is one of New Zealand's foremost jazz singers and, in a wonderful twist of fate, Jay Jackman's father wrote the lyrics to one of his songs.

For Ambrose, surfing is just a selfish act of fun. Riding a piece of foam across the ocean gives him a buzz, and there's nothing quite like feeling that surge of energy pushing him along. He likes everything about being a surfer: the culture, the lifestyle, the people, the history, the fact that you become friends with people of all age groups … Ambrose is good friends with guys in their seventies who are still out there riding waves and he hopes it'll be him in years to come.

'Surfing is my life, and it's a nice life. I like where it's taking me,' Ambrose says.

Cain Aldridge

'School was shaping boards out of plastic rulers; art was drawing surfboards.'

Even as far back as primary school, Cain was 'shaping' at a very basic level. He'd take a 20 cm plastic ruler and, grinding it on the concrete and using a lighter to bend the plastic, pretend to shape a surfboard and then paint it with Twink. Giving each creation away without a second thought illustrates Cain's love of the process, rather than the product. It was all about the shaping and the design, just making something that he loved. He never wanted to run a business; he just wanted to make surfboards. As he started making surfboards, however, the vision for his business grew. It dawned on him that he could actually make a career out of this. At parent-teacher interviews, when asked what he wanted to do when he grew up,

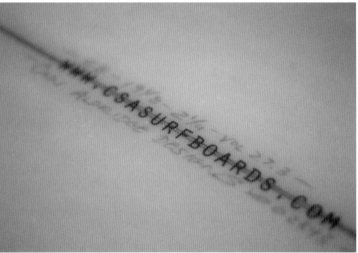

he replied, 'Make surfboards.' When he was told that he couldn't choose this, he simply said, 'Well, that's what I'm going to do.'

Cain would have started his surf journey earlier if his mother had bought him a surfboard. It was all he wanted for Christmas when he was 11 years old. Instead he got a boogie board. He remembers the feeling really clearly: being gutted, but having the foresight to keep it to himself since his family didn't have much of anything. He knew his mum couldn't really afford a surfboard and that she'd thought a boogie board was more or less the same thing. Like a good son he rode his boogie board for a while, but that desire for a surfboard was still burning away inside. The following year, his neighbour sold him a second-hand Goodtime surfboard.

He has so many childhood memories of the water that they all merge into one. Early moments include seeing surfers in the water at Opunake Beach and thinking it was amazing, and borrowing a kneeboard and trying to stand up on it. There were no family ties to surfing; it was simply what he wanted to do. All of this was reinforced by the older surfie guys that Cain looked up to and Opunake being a 'surfie' town. Skateboarding was a natural outlet for his desire to surf, and he would try things out on the surfboard that he could do on his skateboard.

If something of his broke, Cain's first step was to try to fix it, the other option being to not have it any more. Inevitably, his surfboard ended up needed repairing and his natural curiosity for pulling things apart and putting them back together helped start him on the path to eventually making boards. Unsure of the source of resin and fibreglass, he figured it couldn't be that hard to fix his board. A new love was born. It was just as cool to fix and look after his board as it was to ride it. He started fixing all his mates' boards in his bedroom at home. His mum was more than a little concerned about the smell emanating from her 13-year-old son's bedroom.

No one was using the garage so he claimed the space as his workshop and, like many a good Kiwi start-up business, it all grew from there.

The CSA Surfboards factory shop in Taranaki has now exceeded his initial dreams, which were forged by his self-professed small-town mind-set. At the start he simply wanted to make one board, then a couple, until each completed step allowed him to look up and extend his vision. Coming up to creating his 3000th board is testament that Cain is happy to keep expanding that mind-set.

Cain's love for surfboards is evident everywhere in the shop. Watching him show a young grom the new board he has made for him, you see his pride and love for his creation as he chats about the dimensions, the volume and the actual design. This is not a place where boards are pumped out the door purely for profit; it may even be the last consideration. Clearly, Cain wants his board to be loved by its new owner just as much as he loved making it.

His first 1000 boards were hand-shaped. 'I knew nothing about machine shaping when I started, even though it was already being used in the industry.' Now he uses CAD software to create new boards and as a place to store all those initial designs. 'It's cool that you can translate what you do by hand to a machine.'

All his knowledge, years of hard work and templates can be stored now. Cain can repeat and refine boards. 'When I heard about it, I thought, I want one of those things. It's an amazing design tool that's taken my shaping to another level. We can hold people's design files digitally now. They can come back five years later and do a repeat order, or make changes, depending on how they've progressed as a surfer.'

Even with the new machinery and CAD design software, Cain believes that making a surfboard is still an art. Why? Because he claims he knows nothing about science.

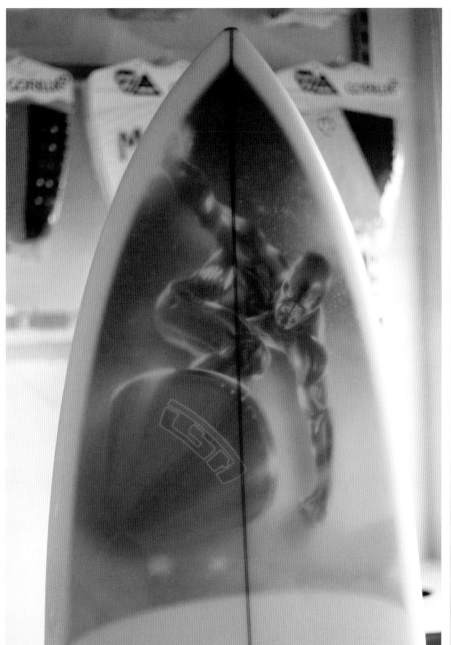

i waihangatia i

AOTE
AROA

made in nz

Tony Ogle

Capturing the Coast on Canvas

Tony can clearly remember sitting on the beach as a 13-year-old, watching a guy catching a wave and thinking, 'I need to do that!'

There are not many things he's still doing 40 years later but surfing is definitely one of them. It's one of the reasons that Gisborne seemed like the natural location for his family, complete with a gorgeous home right on the beach at Wainui. Tony is still surfing several times a week and gets as much of a buzz out of it as he did as a 13-year-old.

His love of the water, the beach and the New Zealand coastline is evident in his art. Tony is a renowned artist who creates stunning prints of New Zealand coastal scenes.

'Surfing is such a healthy pursuit. It generates a real love of the outdoors, and dovetails perfectly with my work as an artist.'

Originally, his plan had been to work from their new house on the beach at Wainui, but the distraction of the waves proved too much.

With a new studio space currently being completed in Gisborne, surfing and his art should soon be back complementing each other again.

Tony's work is full of vibrancy, colour and a love of the outdoors. Only someone who is fully entrenched in beach life and who shares a real love of the ocean could create such emotive work.

'When you enter the water, you enter another zone. Your senses all become tuned to what you are doing with the swell and the waves. You almost hyper-fixate on the water and what it's doing. In between the waves you can relax and chill out, watch the gannets go swooping past. It's about being at one with nature and combining that with the basic thrill of catching a wave — no two ever seem the same. Surfing is about always challenging yourself to try something new, pushing yourself harder and harder.'

It certainly provides Tony with inspiration, a time for reflection, personal challenge and sheer exhilaration. He loves the search for that perfect wave. When all the elements come together to create it — the wind, the bottom contours, and the swell — it's an amazing wave.

Isaac 'Keg' Johnston

'Even a bad surf is a good surf.'

'Keg', as everyone knows him, is a gentle giant of a man with shoulders that look like they have spent a lifetime paddling for waves. This big barrel-chested guy looks more like the former rugby prop he once was than a surfer, but the second you hear him talking about surfing it's obvious how much he loves the sport and his boards. Growing up in Mangawhai, Keg has been surfing since he was about 13. He bought his first board for $80. A 5 ft 11 in New Wave Ralph Blake four-fin, 'it was pretty sweet'.

Keg's passion for surfing spreads like a contagion to everyone he meets. He is a well-known personality on the surfing scene, having competed, judged and even MC'ed the Hyundai Longboard Tour. He took up competition surfing in 2006 while working for Surfing New Zealand, and went on to compete at the Maori Nationals. He placed second to Daniel Kereopa and ending up in Tahiti competing for the New Zealand Maori team.

But it's his collection of boards that really makes Keg stand out. He buys boards that both 'buzz' him, and on which he would like to surf. 'I love my boards; they're gold.' So many of his boards are from the early days of New Zealand surfing, including his Kookbox. It's from the 1920s and is 14 feet, hollow and really similar to old plane wings. It's very heavy and Keg got it off someone whose dad had it sitting in his garage. The two small wooden boards were made from totara in about 1946, after World War Two. A couple of guys used to surf on them out west by Pukekohe. Even though Keg usually does the longboards, his Atlas Woods is a 5 ft 10 in so it's quite a rare one, complete with a seldom-seen decal.

These days, Keg can be found even further north at Ahipara, or 'Shippies', as it's known — Shipwreck Bay, Te Kohanga.

'It's got the second-longest left-hander on the planet when all the conditions link up, so you can get a ride of three to three-and-a-half k's, maybe four, if it's bigger. After one wave I caught at Shippies, it took me forty-five minutes to walk back along the beach. It's just amazing.'

Keg loves nothing better than getting on the water first thing in the morning. A 'dawnie', as they are referred to by surfers, makes for perfect surfing as it's when the earth is cool and there's no wind. Keg reckons he will probably surf until the day he just can't do it any more. 'I just love it. I love the lifestyle. It's a great way to de-stress after work. I'll be doing it until my knees and shoulders give out. There's so much camaraderie and I just dig meeting so many people. So many of my lifelong friendships have come out of surfing.'

I WAIHANGATIA I AOTEAROA · MADE IN NEW ZEALAND ·

Denis Quane

A True Classic

Universally acknowledged as the godfather of New Zealand surfboard manufacturing, Denis Quane had been described by several people as one of the founding fathers of New Zealand surfboard shaping. Whenever his name is mentioned, people smile and talk not only about his boards, but about what a wonderful man he is.

He grew up in Sumner and has lived through the existence of three different Sumner surf clubs. Shifting sand, demolition and then an earthquake saw the demise of the various clubs, but Denis is still standing. He wasn't allowed to join the local surf club until he was 12 so he told a wee fib about his age. They had something called 'Tadpoles' in those days, but 'they never actually did anything'. There was an old surf ski that they could mess around on but it leaked like a sieve so he took it home, fixed it up, and that's how he started shaping.

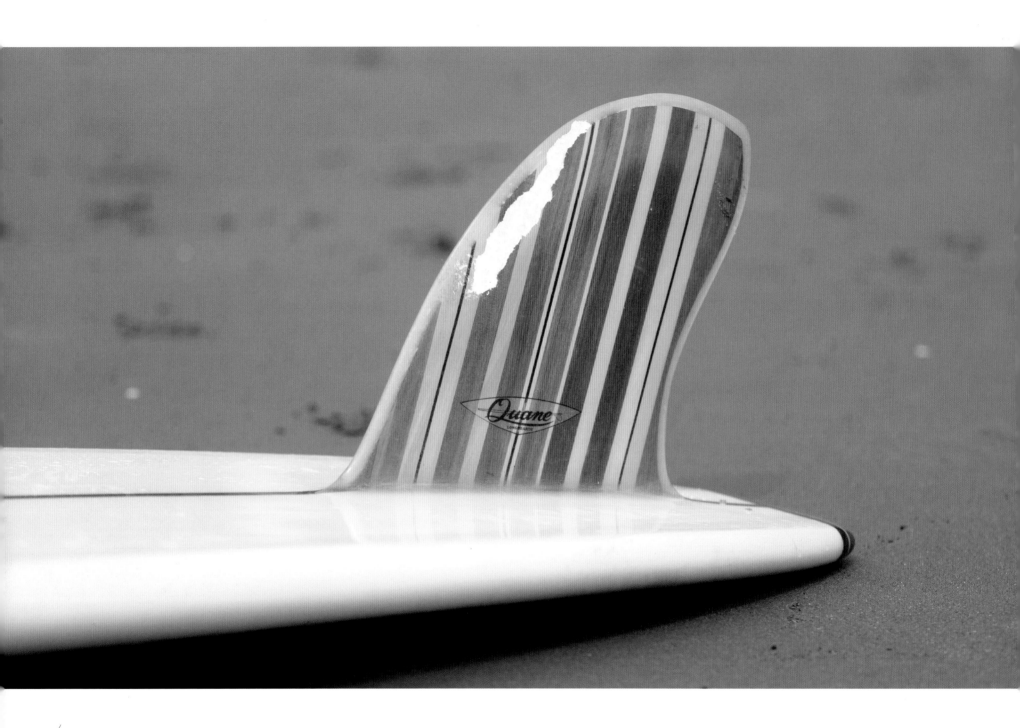

When he was a junior and hadn't yet started competing, he went to Taranaki and saw two guys doing a surf demonstration. It was part of the now-famous visit to New Zealand by Californians Bing Copeland and Rick Stoner, who gave a paddling demonstration on boards they had brought out with them from the States. Inspired by what he had seen, Denis decided to try to build a board like the Californians had been riding. It was the 1950s and he began putting together hollow plywood boards in a workshop in his parents' backyard. After a visit to Australia and witnessing the genesis of foam-board manufacture in Sydney, he decided to start making foam boards. In those protectionist days, it was a battle even to import the right kind of foam.

'You had to have an import licence for everything and they wouldn't give it to me. I ended up having to go to Wellington to the Customs Department and I told them I was not leaving until something happened.' He got the import licence.

Denis has seen the full evolution of surfing in New Zealand. After the initial craze of longboards, the size of boards then dropped pretty dramatically from 9 ft 6 in down to 6 foot. At the same time a lot of Japanese motorbikes started arriving in New Zealand and they proved very popular. A lot of the young men who had been surfing were now riding motorbikes instead. And the drug scene got really bad. A lot of the guys who had been surfing just disappeared from the water. Denis believes that because they were all riding short-boards by then and it took a lot of fitness and work to be able to ride them, fewer people were taking up surfing. The drug culture that entered into surfing gave surfers such a bad name that its popularity really dropped off.

Denis kept making blanks for the various shapers around the country, but it wasn't really until the late 1990s that the longboards started coming back into fashion again. Surfing had also started to become trendy, especially with the popular surf clothing labels like Billabong, Quicksilver and Roxy. They helped bring surfing into the mainstream and the sale of boards took off again.

With 60 years in the longboarding business, Denis shows no sign of wanting to retire yet. He's still surfing and currently planning a new board for himself in a classic longboard style. Quane Surfboards continues to be renowned for its quality. The company's 9 ft 6 in to 9 ft 8 in boards are all hand-shaped and individual.

Denis still enjoys surfing when the weather is good and his health permits. The Christchurch earthquake has thrown up so many challenges over the past few years that surfing has had to take a back seat. A fire in his office space also

caused a lot of problems — hopefully, five years on from the earthquake, they may have a house to live in again.

It's the making of the boards that has always appealed more to Denis than the actual surfing. It has to be a great day on the water to beat shaping a board. These days it's mainly longboards with lots of '60s features. Jay at Sadhana (see page 25) does the glassing and sanding for him, and Denis goes down there to finish them off.

He loves surfing at Sumner, as it's where he's lived and surfed his whole life. He started making boards in the 1950s but his enthusiasm when talking about them even now is obvious. His knowledge and experience can hardly be matched in New Zealand — he's the doyen of shaping. His company slogan is 'True classics don't happen every day', and the same could be said of Denis.

Acknowledgements

When you talk surfing to fellow surfers, their eyes light up and you can see the love of it is never far from the surface. We really appreciate how many people opened up to us about their love affair with the waves, telling us how it's impacted on their lives. We felt very honoured to hear so many personal stories and we hope we have done justice to them all in this book.

Thank you to Bill Honeybone from David Bateman Ltd. I think we go back more than 10 years now and it was great to be able to work closely with you on this project — massive thanks in helping us get it to fruition, and for trusting me when I said it was all under control! Thanks also to Antoinette Sturny and Cheryl Smith for the patient editing and great design work.

And a very special thanks to Georgie. Like most things we do, this was very much a team effort. I just wish surfing was a team sport — maybe we would be better at it! There's nothing I enjoy more than being out on the water with you. Even if it's just sitting, waiting for the next wave, yelling encouragement at each other or sharing the joy when a wave is caught — everything is better when I do it with you.

Jo

Everyone we met was able to recommend others who should be in the book and Volume Two is begging to be written. Particular thanks, though, to Roger Hall, 'Keg', Tony Ogle and Denis Quane for their help in researching and tracking down so many of our surfers. Thank you to our surfing buddy, camera bag holder and general sidekick, Vetchie, for all the many bits and pieces you did for us along the way.

A heartfelt thank you to our gorgeous Taylor and Jacob, who put up with 'just one mummy' far too often while this book was being created, and to Jo's parents who have become cherished grandparents and fantastic babysitters.

I would also like to say a big thank you and *ka pai* to Jo. You spent a lot of hours on the road, working so hard, away from your precious whanau. We wondered if it would be worth it. The project has been fantastic and the end result is definitely worth it. We did it. To poach our wave-riding celebration call — 'Woohoo!'

Georgie

About the authors

Jo Caird has been a photographer for over 20 years. She has photographed a huge range of sporting events, including the Olympics, the Commonwealth Games, the World Cup of Golf, and over eight Rugby World Cup events. Jo has a great reputation as a portrait and event photographer too, but it's her work with the All Blacks that has won her numerous accolades. Together with Georgie, she has now established JOGIE & CO.

Paula George ('Georgie') spent 15 years as an international athlete (netball and rugby) before switching sides of the camera. Since 2005, her focus has been on combining writing with her photography and videography skills, resulting in her position as the behind-the-scenes content provider for AllBlacks.com. Since the All Blacks' victory at the 2011 Rugby World Cup, Georgie has been working on several books, on being a mum, and on learning to surf.